HODDER GCSE HISTORY FOR EDEXCEL

RUSSIA AND THE SOVIET UNION 1917–41

Steve Waugh • John Wright

Although every effort has been made to ensure that website addresses are correct at time of going to press, Hodder Education cannot be held responsible for the content of any website mentioned in this book. It is sometimes possible to find a relocated web page by typing in the address of the home page for a website in the URL window of your browser.

Hachette UK's policy is to use papers that are natural, renewable and recyclable products and made from wood grown in sustainable forests. The logging and manufacturing processes are expected to conform to the environmental regulations of the country of origin.

Orders: please contact Bookpoint Ltd, 130 Milton Park, Abingdon, Oxon OX14 4SE. Telephone: +44 (0)1235 827720. Fax: +44 (0) 1235 400454. Email education@bookpoint.co.uk Lines are open from 9 a.m. to 5 p.m., Monday to Saturday, with a 24-hour message answering service. You can also order through our website: hoddereducation.co.uk

ISBN: 978 1471861970

© Steve Waugh, John Wright 2016

First published in 2016 by
Hodder Education,
An Hachette UK Company
Carmelite House
50 Victoria Embankment
London EC4Y 0DZ

www.hoddereducation.co.uk

Impression number   10 9 8 7 6 5 4 3 2 1

Year   2020 2019 2018 2017 2016

Cover photos © Buyenlarge/Time Life Pictures/Getty Images; To Our Dear Stalin, the Nation, 1949 (litho), Russian School, (20th century) / © Musee de l'Armee, Brussels, Belgium / Patrick Lorette / Bridgeman Images

Illustrations by DC Graphic Design Ltd

Typeset in ITC Legacy Serif Std Book 10/12pt by DC Graphic Design Ltd

Printed in Italy

A catalogue record for this title is available from the British Library.

Acknowledgements

The Publishers would like to thank the following for permission to reproduce copyright material:

Acknowledgements

p.6 *l*, **p.9** *b*, **p.10**, **p.14** *b*, **p.15** *t*, **p.18**, **p.19**, **p.33**, **p.81**, **p.90** *b*, **p.98** *tr*, **p.104** T. Fiehn, *Russia and the USSR* (Hodder Murray, 1996); **p.8**, **p.14** *t*, **p.30**, **p.35** *bl* T. Pimlott, *Russian Revolution* (Macmillan, 1985); **p.15** *b*, **p.16**, **p.120** *b* J. Shuter, *Russia and USSR, 1905–56* (Heinemann, 1996); **p.11**, **p.41** *t*, *b*, **p.46** J. Simkin, *The Russian Revolution* (Spartacus, 1986); **p.22**, **p.23** *tr*, **p.37**, **p.65** *t* M. Lynch, *Reaction and Revolution: Russia, 1894–1924* (Hodder Murray, 2005); **p.23** *l* www.marxists.org/archive/trotsky/1930/hrr/ch08.htm; **p.23** *br*, **p.74** N. Kelly, *Russia and the USSR, 1905–56* (Heinemann, 1996); **p.25** J. Robottom, *Russia in Change 1870–1945* (Pearson Education Limited, 1984); **p.28** *b*, D. Evans and J. Jenkins, *Years of Russia and the USSR, 1851–1991* (Hodder Education, 2001); **p.32**, D. Footman, *The Russian Revolutions* (Putnam, 1964); **p.35** *tl*, **p.48**, **p.63** *t* V. Serge, *Memoirs of a Revolutionary* (Oxford University Press, 1967); **p.35** *tr* R. Pipes, *A Concise History of the Russian Revolution* (Vintage Books, 1997); **p.38** *l*, **p.46** *t*, **p.55** *t*, **p.57** *m*, **p.65** *b*, **p.80**, **p.84** J. Laver, *Russia and the USSR 1905–56* (Hodder Education, 1997); **p.38** *r*, **p.42**, **p.46**, **p.55** *b*, O. Figes, *A People's Tragedy: The Russian Revolution 1891–1924* (Pimlico, 1997); **p.41** *b*, **p.44**, **p.92** *b*, **p.93** *t* R. Radway, *Russia and the USSR 1900–95* (Stanley Thornes Publishers, 1996); **p.46** *b*, J. Daborn, *Russia: Revolution and Counter Revolution 1917–24* (Cambridge University Press, 1990); **p.52**, **p.64**, **p.93** *b* B. Walsh, *Modern World History* (Hodder Murray, 1996); **p.57** *t*, A. White, *Russia and the USSR* (Collins, 1994); **p.57** *b*, **p.59** *t*, **p.63** *b*, **p.69**, **p.75**, **p.76**, **p.120** *t* C. Corin and T. Fiehn, *Communist Russia under Lenin and Stalin* (Hodder Education, 2002); **p.59** *b*, F.W. Stacey, *Lenin and the Russian Revolutions* (Hodder, 1968); **p.63** *m*, H. MacDonald, *Russia and the USSR* (Longman, 2001); **p.67**, **p.98** *tl*, T. Downey, *Russia and the USSR 1900–1995* (Oxford University Press, 1996); **p.82** A. Solzhenitsyn, *The Gulag Archipelago* (Harper Perennial, 2007); **p.83** *tr*, E. Ginsburg, *Within the Whirlwind* (Harvest Press, 1982); **p.83** *bl*, **p.87** *t* F. MacLean, *Portrait of the Soviet Union* (Weidenfeld & Nicolson, 1988); **p.88**, **p.92** *t* J. Brooman, *Stalin and the Soviet Union* (Pearson Education Limited, 1988); **p.90** *t* www.marxists.org/subject/art/lit_crit/sovietwritercongress/zdhanov.htm; **p.105** A. Nove, *An Economic History of the USSR* (Penguin, 1990); **p.98** *bl*, H. Hist and C. Baker, *Russia 1917–45* (Heinemann, 1990); **p.103** *t* M. Sholokov, *Virgin Soil Upturned* (University Press of the Pacific, 2000); **p.103** *b* V. Kravchenko, *I Chose Freedom* (Charles Scribner's Sons, 1946); **p.105** A. Nove, *An Economic History of the USSR* (Penguin, 1990); **p.108** http://spartacus-educational.com/RUSfive.htm; **p.110** *r* J. von Geldern and R. Stites (eds.) *Mass Culture in Soviet Russia* (Indiana University Press, 1995); **p.113** F. Utley, *Lost Illusion* (George Allen & Unwin, 1949); **p.115** S. Fitzpatrick, *Everyday Stalinism* (Oxford University Press, 2000); **p.120** *m* M. Lynch, *Access to History: Stalin and Khrushchev – the USSR, 1924–64* (Hodder Education, 1990).

CONTENTS

Introduction

About the course

During this course you must study four studies:

- A thematic study and historic environment
- A period study
- A British depth study
- A modern depth study.

These studies are assessed through three examination papers:

- In Paper 1 you have one hour and 15 minutes to answer questions on your chosen theme.
- In Paper 2 you have one hour and 45 minutes to answer questions on a depth study and a British period study.
- In Paper 3 you have one hour and 20 minutes to answer questions on one modern depth study.

Modern depth study (Paper 3)

There are four options in the modern depth study unit. You have to study one. The four options are:

- Russia and the Soviet Union, 1917–41
- Weimar and Nazi Germany, 1918–39
- Mao's China, 1945–76
- The USA, 1954–75: conflict at home and abroad

About the book

The book is divided into four key topics:

- **Key Topic 1** examines the revolutions of 1917, including the discontent in Russia at the beginning of 1917, the February Revolution and the abdication of the tsar, the Provisional Government and the Bolshevik Revolution in October.
- **Key Topic 2** explains the Bolsheviks in power in the years 1917–24, including the Civil War of 1918–21, how the Bolsheviks consolidated their power, and the economic, political and social changes that took place in these years.
- **Key Topic 3** concentrates on Stalin's dictatorship and explains the struggle for power in the years 1924–28, the use of terror including the purges under Stalin, the cult of Stalin and propaganda and censorship.
- **Key Topic 4** examines economic and social changes under Stalin especially collectivisation, industrialisation and life in the Soviet Union including the position of women and ethnic minorities.

Each chapter in this book:

- contains activities – some develop the historical skills you will need, others are exam-style questions that give you the opportunity to practise exam skills
- gives step-by-step guidance, model answers and advice on how to answer particular question types in Paper 3
- defines key terms and highlights glossary terms in bold and colour the first time they appear in each key topic.

About Paper 3

Paper 3 is a test of:

- knowledge and understanding of the key developments in Russia, 1917–41
- the ability to answer brief and extended essay questions
- the ability to answer source and interpretation questions.

You have to answer questions in two sections – Section A and Section B. In Section A you have to answer the following types of question:

- **Inference** – making two supported inferences on a provided source.
- **Causation** – explaining why something happened.

In Section B you have to answer a single four-part question, based on two provided sources and two provided interpretations. These enquiry questions include:

- **Utility** – evaluating the usefulness of sources.
- **Interpretation** – explaining what differences there are between two interpretations and why they differ, and making a judgement on a view given by one of the interpretations.

On page 3 is a set of exam-style questions (without the sources). You will be given step-by-step guidance in throughout the book on how best to approach and answer these types of questions.

Paper 3: Modern depth study
Option 30: Russia and the Soviet Union, 1917–41

This is an **inference** question – you have to make two inferences and support each with details from the source.

1 Give two things you can infer from Source A about the Provisional Government. Complete the table below to explain your answer.

  i) What I can infer:

  ....

  ....

  Details in the source that tell me this:

  ....

  ....

  ii) What I can infer:

  ....

  ....

  Details in the source that tell me this:

  ....

  ....

(Total for Question 1 = 4 marks)

This is a **causation** question – which gives you two points which you can use in your answer, although you don't have to. You should develop at least three clear points.

2 Explain why the Bolsheviks won the civil war of 1918–21.

You may use the following in your answer:
- Trotsky
- White commanders

You **must** also use information of your own.

(Total for Question 2 = 12 marks)

This is a **utility** question – it is asking you to decide how useful each source is.

3 (a) Study Sources B and C. How useful are Sources B and C for an enquiry into the effects of industrialisation on the Soviet Union in the years 1928–41? Explain your answer, using Sources B and C and your knowledge of the historical context.

(8)

This is an **interpretation** question – you have to explain one main difference between the two interpretations.

(b) Study Interpretations 1 and 2. They give different views about the effects of industrialisation on the Soviet Union in the years 1928–41. What is the main difference between the views? Explain your answer, using details from both interpretations.

(4)

This is an **interpretation** question – you have to explain why these interpretations differ.

(c) Suggest one reason why Interpretations 1 and 2 give different views about the effects of industrialisation on the Soviet Union in the years 1928–41. You may use Sources B and C to help explain your answer.

(4)

Up to 4 marks of the total for part (d) will be awarded for spelling, punctuation, grammar and use of specialist terminology.

This is an **interpretation judgement** question – you are asked to make a judgement on a view given by one of the interpretations.

(d) How far do you agree with Interpretation 2 about the effects of industrialisation on the Soviet Union in the years 1928–41? Explain your answer, using both interpretations, and your knowledge of the historical context.

(20)

(Total for spelling, punctuation and grammar, and the use of specialist terminology = 4 marks)

(Total for Question 3 = 36 marks)

(Total for Paper = 52 marks)

The revolutions of 1917

This key topic examines the key developments in Russia in 1917, a year in which there were two revolutions. The First World War had increased the unpopularity of Tsar Nicholas II, and he was forced to abdicate as a result of the February Revolution. The short-lived Provisional Government, which followed, was unable to resolve the problems that faced Russia and was overthrown by the Bolsheviks in what became known as the October Revolution.

Each chapter within this key topic explains a key issue and examines important lines of enquiry as outlined in the boxes below.

There will also be guidance on how to answer the interpretations question:
■ Understanding interpretations (page 23)
■ How to answer the first question on interpretations – what is the main difference between the views (page 38).

CHAPTER 1 RUSSIA IN EARLY 1917

■ Threats to the tsarist regime: discontent among peasants and town workers and the growth of opposition.
■ The impact of the First World War, including military defeats, economic, social and political effects, and the Tsar as commander-in-chief.

CHAPTER 2 THE FEBRUARY REVOLUTION

■ Immediate reasons for the February Revolution.
■ Events in Petrograd in February 1917, including strikes and the mutiny in the army.
■ The Tsar's absence and abdication.

CHAPTER 3 THE PROVISIONAL GOVERNMENT

■ The establishment of the Provisional Government and problems it faced.
■ The weaknesses and failures of the Provisional Government, the role of Kerensky and the Bolshevik takeover in October.
■ The significance of the Kornilov Revolt.

CHAPTER 4 THE BOLSHEVIK REVOLUTION

■ Lenin's return and activities including the April Theses and the growth in support for the Bolshevik Party. The 'July Days'.
■ The Bolshevik seizure of power in October 1917 and the reasons for their success. The roles of Trotsky and Lenin.

TIMELINE 1917

25 February	Strikes all over city of Petrograd	**April**	Return of Lenin to Russia and 'April Theses'
27 February	Soldiers in Petrograd garrison desert	**July**	Bolsheviks arrested during the 'July Days'
2 March	Abdication of Nicholas II	**September**	The Kornilov Revolt
3 March	Setting up of the Provisional Government	**October**	Bolshevik seizure of power

1   Russia in early 1917

In 1917 there was massive discontent in Russia, due to long-term economic and political problems made worse by the effects of Russia's military failures in the First World War. These led to growing opposition against Tsar Nicholas II, who was blamed for the military defeats; an opposition which would eventually lead to his downfall.

1.1 Reasons for discontent

In the early twentieth century Russia was a vast empire covering one-sixth of the world's surface (see Figure 1.1). Ruled by Tsar Nicholas II (of the **Romanov dynasty**), it had many different regions and a total population of 125 million people and faced a number of political, economic, social, religious and geographical problems. These led to discontent and growing opposition, which threatened the tsarist regime.

ACTIVITIY ?

Using Figure 1.1, suggest reasons why the size of the Russian Empire made it so difficult to govern.

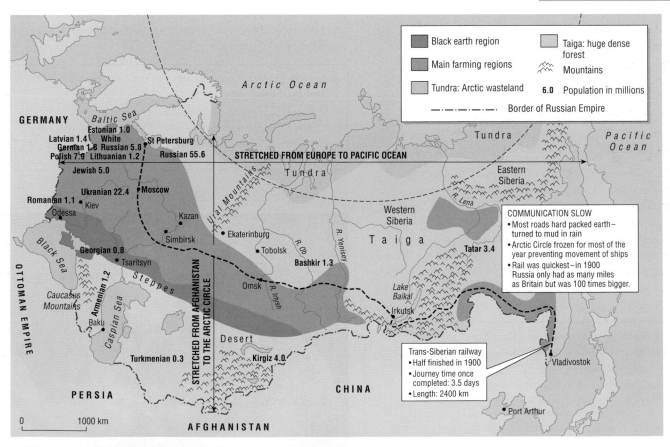

▲ **Figure 1.1** The Russian Empire in the early twentieth century

The 'subject nationalities'

The Russian Empire was difficult to rule because it was made up of more than 20 different peoples or ethnic groups. For six people out of every ten, Russian was a foreign language. These non-Russian groups were known as 'subject nationalities'. Many of these peoples resented being part of the Russian Empire, especially as its rulers carried out a policy of 'Russification'. This meant making non-Russians speak Russian, wear Russian clothes and follow Russian customs. For example, in the area of present-day Poland, it was forbidden to teach children in Polish. Moreover, Russians were often given the important jobs in non-Russian areas.

Discontent with the government

Russia was an autocracy with all the power in the hands of the tsar. The tsar believed that he had a divine right to rule – that is, God had chosen him. This meant he could do whatever he liked without having to consult his people. The only parliament was the *duma* (see page 10) which had very little power.

About 70 per cent of the population were members of the Orthodox Church. The Church was closely linked to the tsar and supported his way of ruling. It taught that the tsar was the head of the country and the Church – in other words, that he was God's chosen representative on earth.

The tsar did have a council of ministers that ran the various government departments, but they could not make important decisions. There were thousands of civil servants, such as tax collectors, who carried out the day-to-day work of government. They were generally poorly paid, so this encouraged bribery and corruption.

The Russian people had little freedom. All unions of workers and strikes were forbidden, and newspapers and books were censored by the government. The tsar was determined to suppress all opposition through the Okhrana, his secret police. They used spies and agents to root out anyone who was against the tsar and his system of government. Such opponents could be imprisoned without trial or exiled to far-off Siberia. Russian writer Leo Tolstoy describes the situation in Source A.

> **Source A** Extract from a letter about the discontent at the time, written from Russian novelist, Leo Tolstoy, to Tsar Nicholas II in 1902
>
> A third of the whole of Russia lives under police surveillance. The army of the police, both regular and secret, is continually growing in numbers. The prisons are overcrowded with thousands of convicts and political prisoners. Censorship has reached its highest level since the 1840s. In all cities … soldiers are … equipped with live ammunition to be sent out against the people.

▶ **Source C** A portrait photo of Tsar Nicholas II of Russia, the Tsarina Alexandra, son Alexis and four daughters – Olga, Tatiana, Maria and Anastasia, c. 1914

Nicholas II's weaknesses

The system of autocracy only worked if the tsar was strong and able to control the government and different nationalities of the vast Russian Empire. Nicholas II, who became tsar in 1894, was not a strong character. He was reluctant to become tsar, possibly because he witnessed the assassination of his grandfather, Alexander II, in 1881. When Nicholas became tsar in 1894 he said:

> What is going to happen to me? I am not prepared to be tsar. I never wanted to become one. I know nothing of the business of ruling. I have no idea of even how to talk to ministers.

Nicholas II insisted on governing as an autocrat. He and his wife, the Tsarina Alexandra, believed that they had been chosen by God to rule and that no one had the right to challenge them. He was ignorant of the nature and extent of opposition to tsarist rule and refused to share power. It was once said that, 'The two most important people in Russia are Tsar Nicholas II and the last person to whom he had spoken'.

Although a devoted husband and father, he was not particularly happy. His only son and heir, Alexis, suffered from an incurable blood disease known as haemophilia and was likely to die young.

> **Source B** Extract from the diary of the tsar's sister, the Grand Duchess Olga
>
> He had intelligence … faith and courage but he was … ignorant about governmental matters. Nicky had been trained as a soldier. He had not been taught statesmanship and … was not a statesman.

Economic problems

Most of the population – 85 per cent – lived in the countryside. Russian agriculture, however, was poor. Extensive tundra, forest and desert meant only about five per cent of the land, mainly in the south-west, was used for farming (see Figure 1.1, page 5). In most villages the land was divided into three large fields. Each household had strips in each of these fields. This scattered strip farming system encouraged **subsistence farming** using primitive hand tools. These old-fashioned farming methods resulted in low food production and frequent famines, such as the one in 1892, shown in Source D.

▲ **Source D** Starving peasants being given food during a famine, 1892

Industrial development

Even though Russia was rich in oil and minerals, **industrialisation** did not happen until the end of the nineteenth century (much later than some other European countries, such as Britain and Germany). Considering Russia's size and resources, its manufacturing output was still very low at the beginning of the twentieth century. Its size and undeveloped system of roads and railways, together with the absence of an effective banking system, all restricted the growth of industry.

Nevertheless, by the outbreak of the First World War in 1914, Russia had experienced a rapid growth in industry due to:

- an increase in the output of coal in the Ukraine
- an increase in the output of oil in the Caucasus
- deliberate government policy.

One of the tsar's ministers, Count Sergei Witte (Minister of Finance, 1893–1903), set himself the huge task of modernising the Russian economy. He invited foreign experts and workers to advise on industrial planning and techniques. His reforms did stimulate industrial growth, as can be seen in Table 1.1. However, rapid industrial growth would in turn lead to poor living and working conditions for workers, causing discontent.

▼ **Table 1.1** Russia's annual industrial production (in millions of tonnes) 1880–1913

	Coal	Pig iron	Oil	Grain*
1880	3.2	0.42	0.5	34
1890	5.9	0.89	3.9	36
1900	16.1	2.66	10.2	56
1910	26.8	2.99	9.4	74
1913	35.4	4.12	9.1	90
1916	33.8	3.72	9.7	64

(* European Russia only)

ACTIVITIES

1 Why do you think the many non-Russian groups in the Russian Empire were known as the 'subject nationalities'?

2 What did 'Russification' mean? Start by defining the term and then give examples of how it was carried out.

3 Study Source A.
   a) Why do you think Tolstoy wrote an open letter to the tsar? What was he hoping to achieve?
   b) Write a letter in response from Nicholas II. Remember that he believed in the system of autocracy and the need to suppress opposition.

4 What was meant when it was said that 'The two most important people in Russia are Tsar Nicholas II and the last person to whom he had spoken'? Why do you think this might have been a problem?

5 What does Source D tell you about life in the Russian countryside and why there might have been discontent?

Practice question

Give **two** things you can infer from Source B about how Russia was ruled in the early twentieth century. *(For guidance, see page 77.)*

ACTIVITIES

1 Study Source F.
   a) What message is the cartoonist trying to put across about Russian society in the early twentieth century?
   b) Do your own sketch to show these different groups. Annotate your sketch with key words to show the main features of the aristocracy, middle class, peasants and town workers.

Practice question

Give **two** things you can infer from Source E about the lifestyle of the wealthy in Russia. *(For guidance, see page 77.)*

Source E Russian writer Leo Tolstoy describes the lifestyle of a Russian nobleman, Prince Dmitri Ivanovich Nechlyudov, in the late nineteenth century

The prince proceeded to a long dining table where three servants had polished for a whole day. The room was furnished with a huge oak sideboard and an equally large table, the legs of which were carved in the shape of a lion's paws. On this table, which was covered with a fine starched cloth with large monograms, stood a coffee pot, a silver sugar bowl, a cream jug with hot cream, and a bread basket filled with freshly baked rolls.

Social problems

Russian society was divided into various classes or groups. The vast majority of the people were poor peasants, while at the other end of the scale, at the top, were the tsar, the **aristocracy** and the higher clergy (the Church leaders who owned large amounts of land). Source F shows a satirical illustration of the hierarchy of Russian society at that time.

The royal family say 'We rule you'

The nobles say 'We govern you'

The clergy say 'We fool you'

The army say 'We shoot you'

The capitalists say 'We do the eating'

The workers at the bottom protest about their lack of freedoms

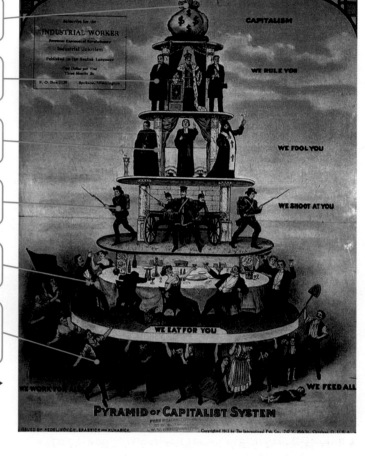

Source F A poster published by the Marxists in 1901 showing their views on Russian society

The aristocracy

The aristocracy made up just over one per cent of the population and yet they owned almost one-quarter of all the land. Some were extremely rich, with lavish homes in the countryside, a second home in a town or city, and many servants, such as described by Russian writer Leo Tolstoy (Source E), and illustrated in Source G.

Source G A dinner party in the palace of Countess Yelisaveta Shuvalova in St Petersburg in 1900

The middle class

By 1914, Russia had a growing **middle class** due to the development of industry. This included bankers, merchants and factory owners. Many made fortunes from government contracts and loans and had a very pleasant lifestyle, eating out at expensive restaurants and frequently going to the theatre or ballet.

The peasants

The biggest, and possibly poorest group, were the peasants. They made up nearly four out of every five Russian people in the years before 1917. For most, life was very hard. They lived in very poor conditions and survived on a staple diet of rye bread, porridge and cabbage soup. When the harvests were poor, there was starvation and disease, as Source H describes. The peasants had a life expectancy of less than 40 years, with many dying from typhus and diphtheria.

> **Source H** A Russian lady, who led a relief party that took food to the Volga region which was suffering from famine in 1892, describes what she witnessed
>
> It was tragedy to see splendid men in the prime of their life walking about with stony faces and hollow eyes. And then there were women clothed only in wretched rags, and little children shivering in the cold wind. There were many of them who had not tasted food for days. It was agonising to hear these people pleading to us for mercy lest they die of starvation. There was no complaint, no cries, just the slow monotonous chant, broken by the sobs of worn out mothers and the cries of hungry children.

The town workers

The final, and most rapidly increasing, group were the new industrial workers in the towns and cities. Large numbers of peasants had flocked to the towns and cities to work in industry. Their conditions were terrible. Workers lived in overcrowded slums (see Source J) and ate cheap black bread, cabbage soup and wheat porridge. In industrial centres away from the cities, workers often lived in barracks next to the factory and slept in filthy, overcrowded dormitories. They earned low wages, worked long hours and were forbidden to form trade unions to fight for better conditions (see Source I). Protests or strikes were crushed, often with great brutality by the police or army.

> **Source I** From *The Story of My Life*, by Father Gapon, written in 1905. Gapon was a priest who organised a trade union to help workers
>
> They receive terrible wages, and generally live in overcrowded conditions. The normal working day is eleven and a half hours not including meal times. But manufacturers have received permission to use overtime. This makes the average day longer than that allowed by the law – fifteen or sixteen hours.

▲ **Source J** A typical flat for workers in the late 1890s

ACTIVITIES ?

1. What do Sources D (page 7), G and J show you about the Russian lifestyle at the beginning of the twentieth century and why there was discontent? Explain your answer.

2. Make a copy of the table below and use the sources and information on pages 6–9 to complete it.
   a) In the second column give a brief explanation for why these group might be discontented.
   b) In the third column explain what you think the tsar should do to reduce or remove this discontent.

	Why discontented	What the tsar should do
Peasants		
Town workers		
Subject nationalities		

3. Go back to Source A on page 6. It gives only an extract from Tolstoy's letter. Using information from your table in Activity 2:
   a) Add another paragraph to his letter about other reasons for discontent in Russia.
   b) Conclude by advising the tsar on what he should do.

Practice question

Explain why there was discontent in Russia in the early twentieth century.

> You may use the following in your answer:
> ■ autocracy
> ■ the peasants
> You must also use information of your own.

(For guidance, see pages 95–96.)

1.2 The growth of opposition

In the years before 1917, there was increasing opposition to Nicholas II for several reasons.

'Bloody Sunday' and the 1905 Revolution

On Sunday 22 January 1905, Father Gapon led a peaceful march of around 200,000 people to the tsar's Winter Palace in St Petersburg. The marchers were petitioning for better working conditions. However, the tsar was not in his palace and the soldiers panicked. They fired on the crowd, killing hundreds and wounding thousands. This event became known as 'Bloody Sunday'. According to an American diplomat at that time, the consequences would be great (Source K):

> **Source K** From a letter by an American diplomat in the Russian city of Odessa writing about 'Bloody Sunday'
>
> Tsar Nicholas has lost absolutely the affection of the Russian people, and whatever the future may have in store for the Romanovs, Nicholas will never again be safe in the midst of his people.

Bloody Sunday, together with discontent over the defeat of Russia in the war with Japan (1904–05), sparked **revolution** in Russia in February 1905. There were strikes and a **mutiny** in the navy. In order to avoid further chaos, Nicholas II issued the October Manifesto, which promised freedom of speech, an end to **censorship** and a national parliament (*duma*). This revolution was a warning to the tsar about the need for change and reform. However, Nicholas ignored this warning.

Stolypin's 'necktie' and the failure of the *dumas*

After the 1905 Revolution, Nicholas appointed Peter Stolypin as prime minister. Stolypin did introduce certain reforms, especially of agriculture and education. However, those who openly opposed the tsar were dealt with severely. There were more than 3,000 executions during Stolypin's time as prime minister – and the gallows became known as 'Stolypin's necktie'.

Moreover, in the years after 1905, Nicholas ensured that the *duma* he had been forced to create had little power. After the election of the first *duma* in 1906, he declared that he had the power to dissolve it, and to change the rules by which it was elected, whenever he liked. There were four different *dumas* in the years 1906–14. Nicholas had gone against the promises made in his October Manifesto, refusing to share power and continuing to rule like an autocrat. This, in turn, stimulated further opposition, particularly among the different political groups (see page 12).

Rasputin

Resentment about the increasing influence of Rasputin was a further reason for the growth of political opposition. After 1907, Nicholas and his wife, Alexandra, came to rely on the help and guidance of a holy man named Gregory Rasputin. Rasputin had the ability to control the life-threatening illness of the tsar's son – Alexei suffered from haemophilia.

Alexandra and Nicholas called Rasputin 'Our Friend' and his position and power at court grew so much that he eventually helped to choose government ministers. Stories about his hedonistic lifestyle abounded, such as rumours of orgies, and there were always large numbers of women in his presence.

Rasputin was another piece of ammunition for those who did not like **tsarism**. These critics saw corruption and incompetence now being added to the list of problems that Russia faced.

Source L From a statement by Rodzianko, Octobrist politician, March 1916, about the evil influence of Rasputin

I said to the tsar – 'This cannot continue much longer. No one opens your eyes to the true role which Rasputin is playing. His presence in Your Majesty's Court undermines confidence in your Supreme Power and may have an evil effect …'

My report did some good – Rasputin was sent away to Tobolsk, but a few days later, at the demand of the Empress, this order was cancelled.

ACTIVITIES

1 What does Source K suggest about the importance of 'Bloody Sunday'?
2 Why was Source M damaging for the tsar's supporters?
3 Devise a caption for Source N that could have been used by opponents of the tsar.
4 Create a table with three columns titled 'Political issues', 'Economic issues' and 'Social issues', then, using the sources and information on pages 10–12, fill in the columns to show how opposition to the tsar was developing in the years before 1917.

Practice questions

1 Give two things you can infer from Source L about Rasputin. (*For guidance, see page 77.*)
2 How useful are Sources L and M for an enquiry into the growth of opposition? Explain your answer, using Sources L and M and your knowledge of the historical context. (*For guidance, see pages 85–87.*)

◀ **Source M** One of the many postcards that circulated around St Petersburg in 1916 and 1917, showing Rasputin and Alexandra

INDUSTRIAL UNREST

As we have seen, Russia's rapid industrial growth had created poor living and working conditions for the industrial workers. This led to a wave of strikes in the years before 1914. One of the most important strikes occurred in 1912 at the Lena goldfields, where troops shot dead more than 200 strikers and injured several hundred (see Source N). The events at Lena heralded a new wave of strikes in urban areas across Russia and there was a general strike in St Petersburg in July 1914.

Source N Some of the ▶ dead strikers at the Lena goldfields, 1912

Threats to the tsarist regime from political groups

By 1917 there were several political groups who opposed the tsar and posed a threat to the tsarist regime through challenging the authority of the tsar.

THE SOCIAL DEMOCRATIC PARTY

Vladimir Lenin

Founded in 1901, the Social Democratic Party followed the teachings of Karl Marx (see Figure 1.2) and believed that the workers (**proletariat**) would one day stage a revolution and remove the tsar. The revolution would lead to the setting up of a communist state. In 1903, the party split into two – **Mensheviks** and **Bolsheviks**. The Mensheviks believed that the party should have a mass membership and were prepared for slow change. The Bolsheviks believed that a small party **elite** should organise the revolution. Vladimir Lenin led the Bolsheviks and the Mensheviks were led by Julius Martov and Leon Trotsky.

THE SOCIALIST REVOLUTIONARIES (SRS)

Alexander Kerensky

Founded in 1901, the SRs, as they were called, believed in a revolution of the peasants and aimed to get rid of the tsar. They wanted to share all land among the peasants, so that it could be farmed in small peasant communities. There was a mixture of beliefs within the party – some wanted to use terror to achieve their aims and others were prepared to use constitutional methods. Terrorist activity by SR members led to the deaths of thousands of government officials in the years before 1917. Alexander Kerensky eventually led the SRs.

THE OCTOBRISTS

Alexander Guchkov

Founded in October 1905, the Octobrists were set up after the tsar issued his October Manifesto (see page 10). They believed that the tsar would carry out his manifesto promises of limited reform. The Octobrists' main area of support came from the middle classes. They were led by Alexander Guchkov.

THE CONSTITUTIONAL DEMOCRATIC PARTY (CADETS)

Paul Milyukov

As Russia developed a middle class, the demand grew for a democratic style of government. Founded in 1905, the **Cadets** wanted to have a **constitutional monarch** and an elected parliament – as in Britain – though some were prepared to set up a republic. The Cadets were led by Paul Milyukov.

> In what ways did these political groups threaten the tsarist regime? **?**

▼ **Figure 1.2** The theory of Marxism

History was shaped by the struggles between different social classes...

As society changed from *feudalism* to *capitalism*, there were struggles between the aristocracy and the middle classes. The middle classes were able to take power from the aristocrats and began to exploit the workers in the new industrial world.

The workers (proletariat) would eventually rebel against their exploitation and set up a socialist state.

Eventually, the ideal state would be created – communism, where everyone was equal and people worked for the good of the commune or state.

...Marx's interpretation of history meant that a successful proletarian revolution could only occur where there was an industrial society.

1.3 The impact of the First World War

When the heir to the Austrian throne, the Archduke Franz Ferdinand, was assassinated in Serbia on 28 June 1914, Austria–Hungary, supported by Germany, declared war on the Serbs. Russia was the protector of Serbia, so Russia mobilised its military forces to help Serbia, leading Germany to declare war against Russia in August.

Russia entered the First World War with great expectations of success. Many believed the sheer size of the Russian army, known as 'the Russian steamroller', would be too strong for both Germany and Austria–Hungary. However, by the end of 1914 Russia had over one million casualties, and by the end of 1916, Russia had suffered defeat after defeat, outlined in Figure 1.3. This led to growing discontent with the tsar and his government.

> **ACTIVITY** ?
>
> Using Figure 1.3, create a timeline of Russian defeats, 1914–16.

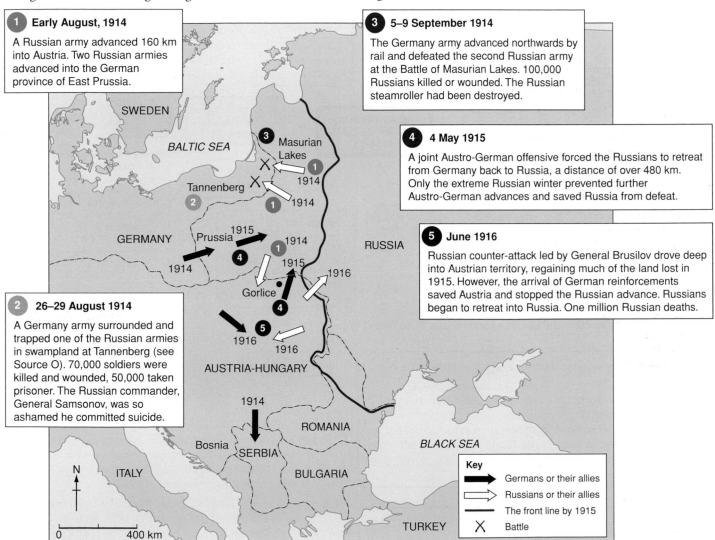

1 Early August, 1914

A Russian army advanced 160 km into Austria. Two Russian armies advanced into the German province of East Prussia.

3 5–9 September 1914

The Germany army advanced northwards by rail and defeated the second Russian army at the Battle of Masurian Lakes. 100,000 Russians killed or wounded. The Russian steamroller had been destroyed.

4 4 May 1915

A joint Austro-German offensive forced the Russians to retreat from Germany back to Russia, a distance of over 480 km. Only the extreme Russian winter prevented further Austro-German advances and saved Russia from defeat.

5 June 1916

Russian counter-attack led by General Brusilov drove deep into Austrian territory, regaining much of the land lost in 1915. However, the arrival of German reinforcements saved Austria and stopped the Russian advance. Russians began to retreat into Russia. One million Russian deaths.

2 26–29 August 1914

A Germany army surrounded and trapped one of the Russian armies in swampland at Tannenberg (see Source O). 70,000 soldiers were killed and wounded, 50,000 taken prisoner. The Russian commander, General Samsonov, was so ashamed he committed suicide.

Key
→ (black) Germans or their allies
→ (white) Russians or their allies
— The front line by 1915
X Battle

▲ **Figure 1.3** The key events on the Eastern Front, 1914–16

Source O The German general, von Moltke, describes the slaughter at Tannenberg

The sight of thousands of Russians driven into huge lakes and swamps was ghastly. The shrieks and cries of the dying men I will never forget. So fearful was the sight of these thousands of men with their guns, horses and ammunition, struggling in the water that, to shorten their agony, they turned the machine guns on them. But even in spite of that, there was movement seen among them for a week after.

Reasons for defeats

The reasons for Russian defeats are shown in Figure 1.4 and the problems of supplies are described in Sources P and Q.

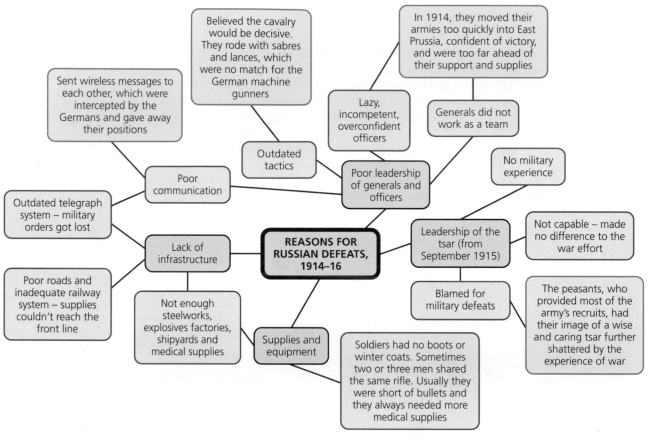

▲ **Figure 1.4** Reasons for Russian defeats in the First World War

Source P From a letter written by the tsar to his wife in July 1916

Without metal the mills cannot supply a sufficient number of bullets and bombs. The same is true as regards the railways. The Minister of Transportation assures me that the railways are working better this year than last, but nevertheless every one complains that they are not doing as well as they might.

Source Q From a letter written by Belaiev, a Russian general, in 1916

In recent battles, a third of the men had no rifles. The poor devils had to wait patiently until their comrades fell before their eyes and they could pick up weapons. The army is drowning in its own blood.

ACTIVITIES

1 Examine Figure 1.4, which shows the key reasons for Russia's defeats.
   a) Explain how the different reasons are linked.
   b) Rank the reasons in order of importance in the defeat of Russia. Explain your ranking (think about the number of links the reasons have to other links in order to explain their importance).

2 You are an adviser to Nicholas II who has been sent to the Eastern Front in September 1915. Write a memorandum to the tsar explaining the problems at the front and what needs to be done. Use Sources P and Q and your work in Activity 1 to help you.

Practice question

How useful are Sources P and Q for an enquiry into Russian defeats in the First World War? Explain your answer, using Sources P and Q and your knowledge of the historical context. *(For guidance, see pages 85–87.)*

Military effects of defeats

Enthusiasm for the war soon waned. Casualties, frequent defeats and poor equipment lowered the morale of the soldiers. They soon lost respect for their officers, who seemed unfeeling and ineffective, and **desertion** was common (see Sources R, S and T). Many soldiers died without weapons or ammunition, and some did not even have boots to wear in the bitterly cold weather.

This discontent spread to the people of Russia. News of high casualties caused alarm in different parts of the Russian Empire. For example, in Baku, the capital of Azerbaijan, women lay on the rails to stop troop trains moving. In other areas there was violent resistance to **conscription**.

> **Source R** From a report by the Chairman of the Military Commission of the *duma*
>
> As early as the beginning of the second year of the war, desertions of soldiers at the front and on their way to the front became commonplace, and the average number of deserters reached 25 per cent. I happen to know of three cases when the train was stopped because there were no passengers on it; all, with the exception of the officer in command, had run away.

> **Source S** A police report on army morale, October 1916
>
> The behaviour of the soldiers, especially in the units in the rear, is most provocative. They accuse the military authorities of corruption, cowardice and drunkenness, and even treason. Everywhere one meets thousands of deserters, carrying out crimes and offering violence to the civilian population.

DIE RUSSISCHE ARMEE LÖST SICH VÖLLIG AUF ..

◀ **Source T** Russian deserters, including officers, in December 1916

Practice question

Explain why there were Russian defeats on the Eastern Front in the years 1914–16.

You may use the following in your answer:
- lack of infrastructure
- leadership of Tsar Nicholas II

You must also use information of your own.

(*For guidance, see pages 95–96.*)

ACTIVITIES ?

1 What does Source S suggest about the behaviour of some Russian soldiers?

2 Does Source R support the evidence of Source S about the behaviour of some Russian soldiers?

3 Study Source T. This photograph was probably taken by opponents of the tsar and the war. Devise a caption that they could have used with this photograph.

15

Economic and social effects of the war

The war had a devastating effect on the Russian economy. Inflation increased – there were seven price rises between 1913 and 1917. Less food was produced because of the shortage of labour and horses. As more peasants were called up to the armed forces, there were fewer men left to work on the land. Indeed, 14 million men were called up to serve in the army between 1914 and 1917. The demand for horses at the front also made it harder for peasants to cultivate their land. This food shortage, in turn, encouraged higher food prices.

Industry, too, was hit by the shortage of workers and by the lack of fuel and essential supplies. Russia's transport system could not cope with the increased demands of war, as well as providing industry with the necessary raw materials. Consumer goods, such as boots and cloth, became scarce and expensive. There were shortages of vital coal, iron and steel. Many factories closed.

The economic problems brought misery. The closure of factories led to unemployment and even greater poverty. Because of the shortages, prices were rising continually, but wages for those still in work were hardly going up at all. To make matters worse, workers were being asked to work longer hours.

All these hardships were, in turn, worsened by fuel and food shortages. Even when fuel and food were available, supplies frequently failed to reach the people in the towns and cities, due to Russia's inadequate transport system and the incompetence of the government.

By the beginning of 1917, Russia was close to defeat on the Eastern Front and there was mass discontent in the armed forces and among the Russian people. To make matters worse, Petrograd (formerly St Petersburg) experienced the worst winter in living memory, with temperatures falling below minus 30 degrees centigrade, at a time when there were severe food and fuel shortages.

> **Source U Police report from Petrograd at the end of 1916**
>
> The industrial proletariat of the capital is on the verge of despair. The smallest outbreak will lead to uncontrollable riots. Even if we assume that wages have increased by 100 per cent, the cost of living has risen by 300 per cent. The impossibility of obtaining food, the time wasted in queues outside shops, the increasing death rate due to inadequate diet and the cold and dampness as a result of the lack of coal and firewood – all these conditions have created such a situation that the mass of industrial workers are quite ready to let themselves go to the wildest excesses of a hunger riot.

Political effects of the war

At first, the war seemed to improve the government of Russia as it encouraged the tsar to work with the *dumas*, but ultimately it seriously weakened the position of the tsar.

The tsar's decision to take over command of the war and move to the front was a serious political mistake. It meant that he left the running of the country in the hands of his wife, Alexandra, the tsarina. She refused to take advice from middle-class members of the *duma* and they became increasingly frustrated.

During the war, the Russian people grew to hate anything German. They changed the name of their capital city from the German St Petersburg to the Russian Petrograd. Alexandra was German and it was rumoured that she was a German spy trying to **sabotage** the Russian war effort.

Rasputin was the only person Alexandra was prepared to listen to. Indeed, he seemed to be in charge of the government. The tsarina frequently dismissed any capable ministers from the *duma* on Rasputin's advice and replaced them with his friends, who were totally incompetent. There were so many changes of ministers that nobody was properly organising food, fuel and other supplies to the cities. The railway system fell into chaos and trainloads of food were left rotting.

As news from the war got worse and the situation in the cities became more desperate, support for the tsar and his wife began to decrease among the middle and upper classes. They blamed the tsar for leaving the country under the control of a German woman, influenced by a mad monk.

DEATH OF RASPUTIN

Rasputin's murder by members of the royal family illustrates the extent of discontent in Russia, especially with Rasputin's influence over Alexandra. Indeed, members of the royal family begged Alexandra to dismiss Rasputin. When she refused, some, led by Prince Yusupov, in desperation decided to assassinate him. One evening in December 1916, Rasputin was invited to Yusupov's mansion for a social evening. During the course of the evening he ate cakes laced with enough cyanide to kill several men. He collapsed but then stood up and ran into the courtyard. There he was shot twice. His hands were bound behind him and his body was thrown into the icy river where he drowned.

You do not need to know the details of his murder for this depth study. However, you may wish to carry out your own further research on the mystery surrounding the exact circumstances of his death.

▲ Nicholas II (on the right) as Commander-in-Chief of the Russian army with other leading generals in 1916. In 1915, Tsar Nicholas II made himself commander-in-chief of the Russian army. As a result, he left St Petersburg and moved to army headquarters in Russian Poland. He was convinced that his direct leadership would increase army morale and improve the war effort. However, Nicholas had little experience or knowledge of military leadership and the military defeats continued. Moreover, in his absence, he left the government of Russia under the control of his wife Alexandra who was increasingly influenced by Rasputin

ACTIVITIES

1 Study Source U. How serious was the situation in Petrograd at the end of 1916?

2 Explain the economic and social effects of the war on Russia in the years 1914–16.

3 In what ways did Nicholas make a political mistake in becoming Commander-in-Chief of the armed forces during the First World War?

4 Look at the circles opposite. This is known as a Venn diagram. They are used to show how factors can overlap with each other – how one factor can influence another. Sketch your own Venn diagram and use it to show the overlap between the military, political, economic and social effects of the war. One example has been done for you, showing the leadership of Rasputin and the tsarina.

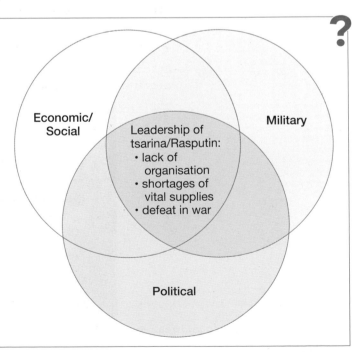

By the beginning of January 1917, the position in Russia was becoming chaotic. Defeats in the war, food shortages and lack of social and political reform meant that support for the tsar had been severely eroded. In Petrograd, in February 1917, there were spontaneous demonstrations against the war. When members of the armed forces joined the demonstrators, the threat to the position of Nicholas II became so serious that he eventually agreed to abdicate.

2.1 Triggers for revolt

The February Revolution was due to both long-term discontent and the growth of opposition, as well as the impact of the First World War (see Chapter 1) and more immediate reasons, particularly the events of the winter of 1916–17.

The situation in Petrograd

By early 1917, it seemed as if the country was on the verge of collapse. It had been hoped that the murder of Rasputin in December 1916 would help to bring some stability to the running of the country – it did not. The winter weather was especially severe in December and January, affecting food supplies to cities and towns. Prices rose (see Table 2.1) and rationing led to further discontent. In Petrograd, there were strikes and people began to demand food.

▼ **Table 2.1** Prices in Petrograd, 1914 and 1916 (figures are in roubles)

Item	1914	1916
Rent for part of a room	2–3 per month	8–12 per month
Dinner in a tea room	0.15–0.20	1 or 2
Tea in a tea room	0.07	0.35
A pair of boots	5–6	20–30
Shirt	0.75–0.90	2.50–3.00

Source A People queuing for bread ▶ in Petrograd in early 1917

Support for Tsar Nicholas continued to diminish, and it seemed like there were no solutions to the many problems facing Russia. The fact that someone like the tsar's brother, the Grand Duke Michael could mention the idea of a direct challenge to the tsar was an indication of the severity of the situation (Source B). Strikes became an everyday occurrence in Petrograd in early 1917, resulting in huge numbers of people on the streets (see Source C). The situation worsened when the soldiers **garrisoned** in Petrograd mutinied and began to take sides with the demonstrators. For Nicholas, this was disastrous.

> **Source B** From a letter written by the Grand Duke Michael to the tsar in January 1917. He was describing the problems facing Russia at that time
>
> The unrest continues to grow. Those who defend the idea that Russia cannot exist without a tsar are losing the ground under their feet, since the facts of disorganisation and lawlessness are obvious. A situation like this cannot last long. It is impossible to rule the country without paying attention to the voice of the people and without meeting their needs.

> **Source C** From a January 1917 *Okhrana* report, describing the mood in Petrograd
>
> The **proletariat** of the capital is on the verge of despair. Time wasted in queues hoping for food to arrive, the increasing death rate due to inadequate diet, cold and dampness as a result of lack of coal and firewood have created a situation whereby the mass of industrial workers are quite ready to let themselves go to the wildest excesses of a hunger riot ... the masses led by the more advanced and already revolutionary minded elements, assume an openly hostile attitude towards the government and protest with all the means at their disposal against the continuation of the war.

Nicholas' presence at the front meant that he did not always know exactly what was happening in Petrograd. In January 1917, General Krymov, a Russian army commander on the Eastern Front, informed Rodzianko, the president of the *duma*, that many soldiers had lost faith in Nicholas and they would support the *duma* if it took over. Krymov also told Rodzianko that Tsarina Alexandra had to be removed from Russian politics. Rodzianko tried to act on this, but he found that Nicholas would not accept advice from him or the *duma*, which had been recalled in 1915. Events rapidly spiralled out of control in February 1917.

ACTIVITIES

1 What can you learn from Sources A, B and Table 2.1 about the situation in Petrograd at the beginning of 1917?

2 Study Source C. List the problems facing:
   a) the people of Petrograd
   b) the Russian government in January 1917.

3 In what ways does Source C help you to understand why many Russians had come to oppose the war by 1917?

? Practice question

How useful are Sources B and C for an enquiry into the discontent in Russia at the beginning of 1917? Explain your answer, using Sources B and C and your knowledge of the historical context. (*For guidance, see pages 85–87.*)

2.2 Events in Petrograd

▼ Figure 2.2 Events in Petrograd, 14–28 February 1917

It was developments in Petrograd in February 1917 that eventually brought about **revolution** and the abdication of the tsar. Figure 2.2 outlines the key events.

Date	Event
14 February	The president of the *duma*, Rodzianko, informs Nicholas that he could no longer rely on his closest supporters in Petrograd.
18 February	A strike at the Putilov engineering works begins. The workers want higher wages because their wages had lost value as a result of inflation.
23 February	International Women's Day organised by socialist groups. Large numbers of women join about 100,000 strikers and demonstrators on the streets of Petrograd. Many women chant simple slogans such as 'Down with hunger!' and 'Bread for the workers!'.
24 February	About 200,000 workers now on strike.
25 February	Strikes all over the city, with about 300,000 demonstrators on the streets. No newspapers are printed and there is no public transport. The police begin to show sympathy for the demonstrators.
26 February	Nicholas instructs the army to restore order but some of the Petrograd garrison had deserted. Some shots are fired on the demonstrators. There are no printers to produce the tsar's proclamations.
27 February	Buildings, shops and restaurants are looted. Most of the Petrograd garrison mutinied and joined the strikers. Nicholas orders the *duma* to dissolve. It does so, but 12 members refuse and set up a 'Provisional Committee'. Alexander Kerensky, a Social Revolutionary, demands that Nicholas abdicate.
	First meeting of the Petrograd Soviet of Soldiers', Sailors' and Workers' Deputies. The Provisional Committee and the Petrograd Soviet are now running the country.
28 February	The Soviet issues the newspaper *Izvestiya* ('The News') and declare its intention to remove the old system of government.

> **Source D** From a letter by a British army officer in Petrograd, February 1917
>
> … as certain as anything that the Emperor and Empress are riding for a fall. Everyone – officers, merchants, ladies – talks openly of the absolute necessity of doing away with them.

▲ **Source E** International Women's Day demonstration, Petrograd, 1917. The banner calls for women to establish an assembly and says 'Freedom for the Citizens of Russia'

▲ **Source F** Soldiers and demonstrators in Petrograd, 25 February 1917. The slogan on the banner reads 'Down with the monarchy'

Source G From the diary of a *duma* deputy, 28 February 1917

Petrograd is without bread, transportation has broken down because of the unusually heavy snow and frosts and principally the war. Ministers have stopped coming to the *duma* ...

Source H Telegrams from Rodzianko, president of the *duma*, to Tsar Nicholas on 26 and 27 February 1917

Telegram of 26 February 1917

The situation is serious. The capital is in a state of anarchy. The government is paralysed; the transportation system has broken down; the supply systems for food and fuel are completely disorganised. General discontent is on the increase. There is disorderly shooting in the streets; some of the troops are firing at each other. It is necessary that some person enjoying the confidence of the country be entrusted immediately with the formation of a new government. There can be no delay. Any hesitation is fatal.

Telegram of 27 February 1917

The situation is growing worse. Measures must be taken, immediately, for tomorrow will already be too late. The final hour has struck, when the fate of the country and the dynasty is being decided. The government is powerless to stop the disorders. The troops of the garrison cannot be relied upon. The reserve battalions of the Guard regiments are in the grips of rebellion, their officers are being killed. Having joined the mobs and the revolt of the people, they are marching on the offices of the Ministry of the Interior and the Imperial *Duma*. Your Majesty, do not delay. Should the agitation reach the army, Germany will triumph and the destruction of Russia along with the dynasty is inevitable.

ACTIVITIES ?

1 What can you learn from Sources F and G about the extent of unrest in Petrograd in 1917?

2 Study Source H, Rodzianko's two telegrams to Tsar Nicholas. Can you suggest reasons why Nicholas failed to respond to the growing problems in Petrograd?

3 Some historians have said that 27 February was the most important day in the Revolution. Why do you think this is the case? Explain your reasons.

The tsar's absence and abdication

The discontent in Petrograd continued through to March 1917 and eventually led to the abdication of the Tsar, as the events in Figure 2.3 outline. Although the absent Tsar decided to try and return to Petrograd, it was too late: the **Romanov dynasty** had reached the point where it ended itself. The abdication of Nicholas and the emergence of the **Provisional Government** out of the *duma* is called the February Revolution. The abdication took place in a railway carriage 320 kilometres from Petrograd (see Source J). The Revolution was over. It had been unplanned and the end of the Romanov dynasty came most unexpectedly.

Date	Event
1 March	The Petrograd Soviet issue Soviet Order Number One, which transfers all authority from army officers to the elected representatives of the soldiers.
2 March	Nicholas decides to return to Petrograd and is met at Pskov, where his leading generals tell him that his presence in the capital will do no good. They advise him to abdicate. Nicholas abdicates and refuses to nominate his son Alexei as his successor, because of his haemophilia. Nicholas' brother, the Grand Duke Michael, is then proposed as the new tsar, but he declines.
3 March	The Provisional Committee renames itself the Provisional Government and becomes responsible for running the country.

▲ **Figure 2.3** Events in Petrograd, 1–3 March 1917

Source I From *The History of the Russian Revolution* by Leon Trotsky, published in 1930

It would be no exaggeration to say that Petrograd achieved the February Revolution. The rest of the country adhered to it. There was no struggle anywhere except in Petrograd. Nowhere in the country were there any groups of the population, any parties, institutions or military units ready to put up a fight for the old regime. Neither at the front nor at the rear was there a brigade or regiment prepared to do battle for Nicholas II. ...Thus ended a reign which had been a continuous chain of ill luck, failure, misfortune, and evil-doing, from the shooting of strikers and revolting peasants, the Russo–Japanese war, the frightful putting-down of the revolution of 1905, the innumerable executions and ending with the insane and contemptible participation of Russia in the insane and contemptible world war ...

ACTIVITIES ?

1 What can you learn about the abdication of Nicholas II from Source J?

2 Construct a flow chart showing the events in Petrograd of February–March 1917 leading to the abdication of the tsar.

3 Re-read Chapters 1 and 2 (pages 5–22). What were the causes of the February Revolution? Make a list of the causes under the headings below. Then highlight what you think are long- and short-term causes in different colours.
   ■ Impact of the war
   ■ Social problems
   ■ Mistakes of the tsar
   ■ Economic problems
   ■ Political problems

Practice question

Explain why Nicholas II abdicated in March 1917.

You may use the following in your answer:
   ■ Effects of the First World War
   ■ Army mutiny
You must also use information of your own.

(For guidance, see pages 95–96.)

▲ **Source J** The abdication of Nicholas II, March 1917. Nicholas is seated

2.3 What are interpretations of history?

You will have to answer three questions about interpretations in the examination. These are:

1 What is the main difference between these interpretations?
2 Why are these interpretations different?
3 How far do you agree with the view given by one of the interpretations?

An interpretation of history is a view given of the past – an event, movement, the role of an individual and so on – written at a later date. It could be a view given by an historian, from a textbook, from a history website. The writer has the benefit of hindsight and is able to consult a variety of sources of evidence to give their view of what took place.

There are different interpretations about a past event or person because the writer could focus on or give emphasis to a different aspect of a past event or person, or may have consulted different sources from the past. The writer will carefully choose words and select or omit certain details to emphasise this view. The fact that there are different interpretations of the past does not necessarily mean that one of them is wrong. The two writers might simply have used different sources but they might also have used the same sources and reached different conclusions.

Your first task is to identify the view that is given by the interpretation of the event or person. Here is an interpretation of the causes of the February Revolution.

> **Interpretation 1** From *The History of the Russian Revolution Volume One: The Overthrow of Tzarism* by Leon Trotsky, published in 1930
>
> To the question, who led the February Revolution? We can then answer definitely enough: Conscious and well-organised workers educated for the most part by the Bolshevik Party of Lenin. But we must here immediately add: This leadership proved sufficient to guarantee the victory of the revolution, but it was not adequate to transfer immediately into the hands of the proletariat town workers the leadership of the revolution.

The view that is given here is:

This interpretation gives the view that the February Revolution was the work of the Bolshevik Party led by Lenin who had prepared the workers for such a revolution. It uses phrases such as 'well-organised workers' who were educated 'by the Bolshevik Party of Lenin' to show this view.

Here is a second interpretation of the February Revolution.

> **Interpretation 2** From *Reaction and Revolution: Russia, 1894–1924* by Michael Lynch, published in 1992
>
> The February Revolution owed almost nothing to Bolshevik influence. Hardly any of the Bolshevik leaders were present in Petrograd, or indeed in Russia, at the time. Lenin and a group of senior Bolsheviks were in Switzerland and Bukharin and Trotsky were in the USA. It is small wonder, then, that the events of February took them by surprise. The revolution was the work of workers and soldiers in Petrograd acting on their own initiative.

And here is a third interpretation of February Revolution.

> **Interpretation 3** From *Russia and the USSR, 1905–1956* by Nigel Kelly, published in 1996
>
> The final overthrow of the tsar happened more by chance than by any great plan. Indeed the February Revolution broke out because of the severity of the Russian winter. The first three months of 1917 were much colder than usual, with temperatures averaging -12 degrees centigrade. The Russians were used to cold weather, but on top of food shortages due to the First World War, it was too much for many people especially in Petrograd.

ACTIVITY

Read Interpretation 1 and the information underneath it. This outlines the view it gives on the February Revolution and the evidence it uses. Now try answering the questions below on Interpretations 2 and 3 in a similar way.

Interpretation 2	
1 What view does it give about the February Revolution?	
2 What evidence from the interpretation supports this view?	
Interpretation 3	
3 What view does it give about the February Revolution?	
4 What evidence from the interpretation supports this view?	

You will be given advice on pages 38, 46–47 and 55–56 on how to answer interpretation questions

3 The Provisional Government

After Tsar Nicholas II abdicated in early March a Provisional Government was set up to run Russia until elections could be held. Although the Provisional Government initially had some successes, it was short-lived because it failed to deal with the problems facing Russia and made the fateful decision to continue involvement in the First World War. As conditions deteriorated on the home front, and the Russian armies continued to suffer defeat after defeat, support for the Provisional Government fell away.

3.1 The establishment of the Provisional Government

The end of **tsarism** was unplanned and took people by surprise. On 3 March 1917, the **Provisional Government** was set up to govern until elections for a **Constituent Assembly** (parliament) could be held, and a permanent government established.

The Provisional Government consisted of a **cabinet** of ministers. The prime minister was Prince Lvov, a wealthy aristocratic landowner, and other leading figures included:

- Milyukov – Foreign Minister and leader of the **Cadets**
- Guchkov – War Minister and leader of the Octobrists
- Kerensky – Minister of Justice and a Social Revolutionary.

The remaining ministers were chosen from the Octobrist and Cadet parties. Thus, the new government was composed of middle-class politicians who wanted to draw up a **constitution** and establish a democratic government. Initially, the **Bolsheviks** supported it, as they believed that the **working classes** could become better organised under such a government. Then, in the future, they thought workers would be able to seize power from the **middle classes**.

The Provisional Government's reforms

The Provisional Government did make some of its promised reforms during the early weeks of its ministry; many were pushed through by Alexander Kerensky, who won great personal support for his powerful speeches. They included:

- Freedom of religion
- Freedom of speech
- Recognition of trade unions
- Introduction of an eight-hour day for industrial workers
- Promise of an elected parliament
- Abolishment of secret police
- **Amnesty** for political prisoners.

Each reform tried to address problems which had either not been solved after the 1905 **Revolution**, or had been created by the tsar and his ministers in an effort to keep tight control over the Russian people. The reforms were quite wide-ranging and it was hoped that they would satisfy the workers and the middle classes.

The Provisional Government's problems

Nevertheless, the Provisional Government faced a number of problems as soon as it was formed:

- it was not a truly elected body and did not represent the people of Russia
- there were defeats in the war
- soldiers were deserting
- peasants were looting the property of the landlords and seizing their land
- soldiers and workers were setting up elected councils of workers, known as **soviets**, in towns and cities
- people wanted an end to food shortages
- some of the subject nationalities (see page 5), such as the Poles and Finns, were hoping that there might even be a chance of independence in the near future.

ACTIVITIES

1 Look at the list of the problems that faced the Provisional Government. Organise them into the categories below and then number them in what you think is their order of importance.

Political problems	Economic problems	Military problems

2 Now look at the list of the Provisional Government's reforms. Using your work in Activity 1, choose the three most important for addressing the problems Russia faced in 1917 and explain each choice.

3.2 Weaknesses and failures of the Provisional Government

Perhaps the most serious issue facing the Provisional Government was the formation of the Petrograd Soviet of Workers' and Soldiers' Deputies. By early March, the **Soviet** had about 3,000 elected members and contained many revolutionaries, especially Socialist Revolutionaries and **Mensheviks** (see page 12). The existence of the Provisional Government and the Petrograd Soviet meant that there were two bodies running Russia; known as the Dual Authority. Both bodies met in the same building, the Tauride Palace. Initially they worked together – indeed Kerensky was a member of both. However, as the months wore on, a gulf between the two began to grow. The Soviet came under the influence of the Bolsheviks, who attacked the Provisional Government for continuing the war. The Soviet only wished to see the German army pushed out of Russia, whereas the Provisional Government was prepared to fight on with Britain and France until Germany surrendered.

Soviet Order Number One

In March 1917, the Petrograd Soviet issued Soviet Order Number One (see Source A). This meant that the orders of the Provisional Government were only binding in regards to military affairs if they were approved by the Soviet. This significantly weakened the new government's authority.

> **Source A** Soviet Order Number One, 14 March 1917
>
> The Soviet of Workers' and Soldiers' Deputies has resolved:
> - In all its political actions, troop units are subordinate to the Soviet.
> - All types of arms must be kept under the control of the company and battalion committees and in no case turned over to officers, even at their demand.
> - The orders of the State *Duma* shall be executed only in such cases as do not conflict with the orders of the Soviet of Workers' and Soldiers' Deputies.

Practice question

Give **two** things you can learn from Source A about Soviet Order Number One. (*For guidance, see page 77.*)

◀ **Source B** The Petrograd Soviet meeting in early 1917. Sometimes as many as 3,000 soldiers and workers attended these early meetings

Defeats in the war

Despite Soviet Order Number One, the Provisional Government decided to continue the war because it was concerned at the heavy demands Germany would make if Russia made peace. Alexander Kerensky, now the Minister for War, visited the troops and persuaded them to support a new June offensive. Surprisingly the Petrograd Soviet agreed and supported Kerensky's offensive in the hope it would drive the German forces out of Russia. There were even some Bolsheviks – Stalin and Kamenev (see page 73) – who felt that the war should not be stopped.

However, the decision to continue the war was fatal for the Provisional Government as further defeats served only to increase its unpopularity, weakening it further. Kerensky's June offensive was a failure and resulted in more than 60,000 deaths and yet more desertions.

To add to the misery of the Provisional Government, Germany sent exiled revolutionaries back to Russia in the hope that they would stir up rebellion. Among these was Lenin, the Bolshevik leader, who arrived in Petrograd in April 1917 (see page 30). Lenin began to call for the overthrow of the Provisional Government.

Nevertheless, the first meeting of the **All-Russian Congress of Soviets** gave a vote of confidence to the Provisional Government in June 1917. The Congress consisted of the representatives from the newly created soviets which had been set up at local level all over Russia after the February Revolution. Only 105 out of 822 representatives in the Congress were Bolsheviks.

The July days

Despite the vote of confidence, by July, the Provisional Government was still experiencing problems. The war was not going well and the growing power of the soviets and strength of opposition were key concerns. The sharing of the Dual Power was coming under increasing strain. The Austrian Front was disintegrating and this caused many soldiers to flood back to Russia. For three days (July 3–6), there was chaos in Petrograd when the soldiers and some Bolsheviks tried to overthrow the Provisional Government. These are known as the 'July Days'. The riots and disorder were only restored when Kerensky, the Minister of War, was able to move loyal troops to quash the rebels (see Source C). About 400 people were killed and injured and Lenin fled the country (see page 31).

▼ **Source C** Demonstrators in Petrograd being fired upon by government troops during the July Days, 4 July 1917

Alexander Kerensky was appointed the new prime minister on 8 July 1917. He had cemented his position as the most powerful politician in Russia. He was determined to continue the war and wait until the elections before any decisions would be made about ending Russia's participation. However, there was growing disquiet among many Russians because little seemed to have changed since the abdication of Tsar Nicholas (see Source D).

> **Source D** From *Worker and Soldier*, a pro-Bolshevik newspaper, August 1917
>
> The Kerensky government is against the people …
> The people can only be saved by the completion of the revolution, and for this purpose the full power must be in the hands of the soviets.
>
> - All power to the soviets
> - Immediate truce on all fronts
> - Landlord estates to the peasants
> - Workers' control over industrial production
> - A Constituent Assembly

ACTIVITIES ?

1 In what ways is Source C helpful in understanding the 'July Days'?
2 Study Source D. What criticisms was the newspaper making about the Provisional Government?
3 What does Source E show about Kerensky in 1917?

▲ **Source E** Kerensky visits troops, 14 July 1917

ALEXANDER KERENSKY, 1881–1970

1881	Born in Simbirsk
1899	Attended St Petersburg University. Gained a law degree
1905	Jailed on suspicion of belonging to a militant group. Afterwards worked as a defence lawyer in a number of political trials of revolutionaries
1912	Elected to the Fourth *Duma* as a member of the Trudoviks, a moderate labour party
1917 March	Minister of Justice on the Provisional Government. Responsible for introducing basic civil liberties such as freedom of speech, press, assembly and religion, universal suffrage and equal rights for women
1917 March	Elected vice-chairman of the Petrograd Soviet
1917 May	Appointed Minister of War in the Provisional Government
1917 July	Appointed Prime Minister of the Provisional Government
1917 August	Appointed Commander-in-Chief of the armed forces
1917 November	Fled to France after Bolshevik Revolution
1970	Died in exile in New York

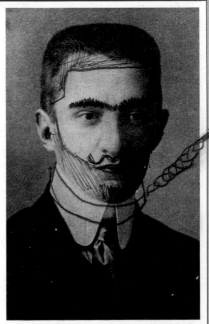

3.3 The Kornilov Revolt

After the 'July Days', it seemed as if the Provisional Government was in control – but it was not. This was shown in the Kornilov Revolt. General Kornilov, the new Supreme Commander-in-Chief of the Russian armed forces, threatened to seize power in Petrograd. There is some debate about the events surrounding the Revolt but some points are clear.

By the end of August, German forces had advanced far into Russia and began to threaten Petrograd. A large number of deserters and refugees flooded into the city, heightening the sense of crisis. Kornilov declared if Russia was to defeat Germany, there had to be stability at home. He would help to restore order and ensure that there was no anarchy or socialist-style government in Russia (see Sources F and G). Kornilov did not agree with the Petrograd Soviet's wish to end the war and he sought to set up a military dictatorship.

> **Source F From a speech by Kornilov in August 1917**
>
> It is time to hang the German supporters and spies, with Lenin at their head, and to disperse the Soviet of Workers' and Soldiers' Deputies far and wide. I have no personal ambition, I only wish to save Russia, and will gladly submit to a strong Provisional Government purified of all undesirable elements.

> **Source G From General Kornilov's telegram to Kerensky, 27 August 1917**
>
> People of Russia! Our great motherland is dying. I, General Kornilov, declare that under pressure of the Bolshevik majority in the soviets, the Provisional Government is acting in complete accord with the plans of the German General Staff. It is destroying the army and is undermining the very foundations of the country. The heavy sense of the inevitable ruin of our country forces me to call upon all the Russian people in these terrible times to come to the aid of the dying motherland.

Kornilov decided to march on Petrograd to save the Provisional Government. (There is some evidence to show that Kerensky asked Kornilov to march on Petrograd but then changed his mind when he realised Kornilov intended to set up a military dictatorship.) To win support and clearly explain his aims, Kornilov issued a manifesto which:

- attacked the Bolsheviks in the Petrograd Soviet
- asked for the war to be continued
- called for the meeting of a **Constituent Assembly**.

Kornilov was immediately condemned by Kerensky, and Petrograd was placed under **martial law**. As Kornilov and his forces approached Petrograd, Kerensky allowed the Bolshevik **Red Guards** to arm and was happy to see the Bolsheviks persuade many of Kornilov's troops to desert. Kerensky also set free many Bolsheviks who had been imprisoned after the July Days, so that there would be a considerable force to oppose Kornilov in Petrograd.

Railway workers prevented Kornilov's troops from approaching Petrograd and printers stopped publication of newspapers that supported the revolt. The attempted revolt failed and Kornilov was arrested.

Practice questions

1 How useful are Sources D (page 27) and F for an enquiry into problems faced by the Provisional Government? Explain your answer, using Sources D and F and your knowledge of the historical context. (*For guidance, see pages 85–87.*)
2 Explain why the Provisional Government faced problems.

You may use the following in your answer.
- The Petrograd Soviet
- The Kornilov Revolt

You must also use information of your own.

(*For guidance, see pages 95–96.*)

▲ **Source H** An outpost of military units fighting against General Kornilov, Petrograd, August 1917

Significance of the revolt

With the arrest of Kornilov, the Army High Command had lost its commander-in-chief and morale sank even lower. Moreover, officers continued to be murdered and desertions reached an even higher level. The army was no longer in a position to set up a military dictatorship.

Kerensky's government looked rather weak and the Bolsheviks, who had secured control of the Petrograd Soviet, were strengthened and in the ascendancy. They could show that they had helped save Petrograd. Many of their followers were armed and those imprisoned in July were freed – the

Bolsheviks began to sense that their time was approaching. Therefore Lenin began to make plans for his return from exile.

All the problems that the Provisional Government had faced in March had not gone away and by October it retained little authority. The Bolsheviks' promises (see page 31) were proving more attractive than the seeming inaction of Kerensky. It is ironic that when Kerensky did act – setting the date for Constituent Assembly elections – it pushed Lenin to decide on a takeover. Lenin said the Provisional Government was 'ripe for the plucking'.

ACTIVITIES

1 Study Sources F and G. What were Kornilov's aims?

2 Why did the Kornilov Revolt fail?

3 Re-read pages 24–29. Why was the Provisional Government in a weak position by 1917? Answer by constructing a diagram as opposite, with the most important reasons at the top and moving in a clockwise direction.

4 Revisit your work on the problems Tsar Nicholas II faced (pages 5–22) and those of the Provisional Government (pages 24–29). You will notice they faced similar problems. Copy the table below and complete the boxes, explaining your answer.

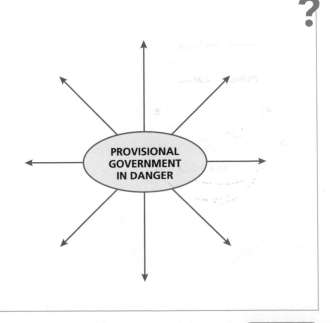

PROVISIONAL GOVERNMENT IN DANGER

Problem	Worse for Tsar Nicholas II?	Worse for Provisional Government?

4 The Bolshevik Revolution

The Bolshevik Party seized power in October 1917 with very little opposition. The Provisional Government was removed with ease and Lenin established a government based on the ideas of Karl Marx (see page 12). Although the Bolshevik Party had been quite insignificant before 1905, membership did begin to grow slowly thereafter. The leading Bolsheviks were determined and dedicated and never lost sight of their goal – a revolution that would bring power to the working classes. The First World War created the opportunity for their success.

4.1 Lenin's return and activities before the Revolution

When war broke out in 1914, Lenin was in Poland. He was arrested for being Russian, but then allowed, with Austrian help, to travel to Zurich in neutral Switzerland. Utterly opposed to the war, he and fellow Bolsheviks were condemned as traitors by Russia and forced into exile. Moreover, many socialists in Europe supported the war, seeming to show that Lenin and his fellow Bolsheviks were out of step with current thinking.

After the February Revolution in 1917, Lenin was desperate to return to Russia. He was keen that his supporters at home should put forward the message that the Bolsheviks wanted peace and an end to the chaos in Russia. As we have seen (page 29), the Germans decided to help Lenin return from exile in Switzerland, in the hope that he would overthrow the new government in Russia. The Germans thought that if Russia pulled out of the war, then more troops could be moved to the Western Front to fight Britain and France. Lenin was put in a sealed train and sent across Germany and Sweden. He arrived in Petrograd at the Finland Station on 3 April 1917 (see Sources A and B). The price he paid for this method of transport was the accusation that he was a German spy, in the pay of the enemy. Lenin was unconcerned. He had returned and, moreover, the money from the Germans would help finance his revolution.

> **Source A** From the *Memoirs of Lenin* written by N. Krupskaya (Lenin's wife), published in 1970. Here she is describing Lenin's arrival at the Finland Station
>
> The Petrograd masses, workers, soldiers and sailors came to meet their leader … There was a sea of people all around. Red banners, a guard of honour of sailors, searchlights from the fortress of Peter and Paul decorated the road … armoured cars, a chain of working men and women guarded the road.

◀ **Source B** A 1930s painting of Lenin's arrival at the Finland station in 1917

The April Theses

Lenin made it clear to his followers that he would not support the **Provisional Government**. He wanted a workers' revolution and his plans were set out the day after his return, in what became known as the April Theses.

THE APRIL THESES

i) The war with Germany had to end.

ii) Power had to pass from the middle classes to the working classes.

iii) All land had to be given to the peasants.

iv) The police, army and bureaucracy should be abolished.

v) The capitalist system had to be overthrown by the workers – banks, factories and transport should be nationalised.

vi) The Bolsheviks should take control of the Soviets in order to achieve their aims. The slogan 'All power to the Soviets' became the watchword.

The Bolsheviks did grow in popularity. Membership had grown from 24,000 in February to 100,000 in April. By June 1917, there were more than 40 newspapers spreading Lenin's views and ideas across Russia. The Bolsheviks even had their own 'Red Guard' – by July, there were about 10,000 armed workers in Petrograd itself.

The impact of the 'July Days'

By July, Lenin felt that the Bolsheviks had grown sufficiently to challenge the Provisional Government, who had done little to put right the grievances of the people. The 'July Days' were not a success for the Bolsheviks (see page 26).

Kerensky, now Prime Minister, accused the Bolsheviks of being German spies, because he knew that Lenin's return to Russia had been financed by Germany. Moreover, much of the Bolsheviks' revolutionary activity since April had been backed by German money. Lenin fled the country and other leading Bolsheviks were arrested or went into hiding, denounced as traitors. Their newspaper, *Pravda*, was closed down. It appeared that the Bolsheviks' chance to seize power had gone and that the Party was in decline.

However, the Bolsheviks were not finished. Lenin directed them from Finland and they were able to continue to function and maintain their high profile. Lenin altered the views he held before 1917 that the peasants would not play a significant role in any future revolution. He accepted land seizures and encouraged even more, thus winning support in the countryside. The slogan 'land to the peasants' was taken up by the Bolsheviks.

Furthermore, Lenin knew that the Russian army could be swayed towards the Bolshevik anti-war policy – the majority of soldiers were really 'peasants in uniform'. The new slogan of 'Peace, Bread, Land' began to attract more and more followers during these critical times.

ACTIVITIES

1 What can you learn from Source B about the attraction of Lenin in 1917?

2 Construct a table like the one below and explain why each group would support or oppose the April Theses.

Group	Support the April Theses	Oppose the April Theses
Workers		
Middle classes		
Peasants		
Soldiers		

3 Why were the July Days important for the Bosheviks? Give reasons for your answer.

Practice questions

1 Give two things you can infer from Source A about Lenin's arrival in Russia. (*For guidance, see page 77.*)

2 How useful are Sources A and B for an enquiry into Lenin's return to Russia in April 1917? Explain your answer, using Sources A and B and your knowledge of the historical context. (*For guidance, see pages 85–87.*)

4.2 The Bolshevik seizure of power

Despite Lenin's exile, the Bolsheviks continued to grow in popularity. Membership grew from 100,000 in April to 340,000 in October, with 60,000 members in Petrograd alone. Their role in suppressing the Kornilov Revolt (see page 28) helped increase their popularity – they were able to say they were the true defenders of Petrograd. Moreover, the Red Guard had retained the weapons given to them by Kerensky during the revolt.

The move to revolution

The **All-Russian Congress of Soviets** was due to meet in late October and it was possible that the Bolsheviks would not have a majority of representatives in it. If, however, the Bolsheviks overthrew the Provisional Government before this, they could present their new authority as a *fait accompli*, which the Congress would find difficult to reject.

Furthermore, Lenin was also aware that the Bolsheviks were unlikely to win a majority of seats in the **Constituent Assembly** elections that Kerensky had called (see page 29). He knew that if they were in power before these elections, then the results could be ignored if they were unfavourable to the Bolsheviks.

Lenin started calling for a revolution, but he still remained in exile in Finland. In September he wrote:

> History will not forgive us if we don't assume power.

Lenin finally returned to Petrograd on 7 October and then went into hiding. On 10 October, he persuaded the Bolshevik **Central Committee** to agree in principle to an uprising, but two influential leaders – Kamenev and Zinoviev – voiced strong objections. These two published their objections in a newspaper, alerting Kerensky to the Bolshevik threat. Lenin was furious.

On 23 October, Kerensky tried to remove the Bolshevik threat – he closed down the Bolshevik papers (**Pravda** and *Izvestiya*) and attempts were made to round up leading Bolsheviks. The Bolsheviks were forced into action and Lenin ordered the revolution to begin before Kerensky could capture them. Thus, inadvertently Kerensky had decided the exact timing of the revolution – 24 October.

All the problems that the Provisional Government had faced in February had not gone away and by October it retained little authority. Lenin's promises of 'Peace, Bread, Land' were proving more attractive than the seeming inaction of Kerensky. It is ironic that when Kerensky did act – setting the date of the elections for the Constituent Assembly for November – it pushed Lenin to decide on a takeover.

Interpretation 1 From *The Russian Revolution* by D. Footman, published in 1962

After the Kornilov Revolt, Kerensky and his cabinet were still in power. But there had been a striking change in the mood throughout the country. The Bolsheviks could now claim to have been the leaders in the 'victory over the counter-revolution' and their power and influence increased rapidly.

ACTIVITIES ❓

1 Create a timeline showing the development of the Bolshevik Party from April to October 1917.

2 Read Interpretation 1 and answer these questions:
   a) What view does it give of the Provisional Government?
   b) What evidence from the interpretation supports this view?

3 Why did Kerensky think it important to close down the Bolshevik newspapers in October?

Practice question

Explain why Lenin decided to begin the revolution in October 1917.

You may use the following in your answer:
■ The Kornilov Revolt
■ The Constituent Assembly elections

You must also use information of your own.

(For guidance, see pages 95–96.)

Events of the Revolution

On the night of 24 October the Bolsheviks captured key buildings, such as telegraph offices and railway stations, and road blocks were set up on the city's bridges and roads surrounding the Winter Palace, where the Provisional Government was in session. There was little resistance and the citizens of Petrograd went about their everyday business.

> **Source C** Lenin, on the eve of the Bolshevik Revolution, urging his colleagues to do what in fact they were doing!
>
> The situation is extremely critical. Delaying the uprising now really means death … We must at any price, tonight arrest the Ministers and we must disarm the military cadets … We must not wait! We may lose everything! … The government is tottering. We must deal it the death blow at any cost.

Kerensky escaped from Petrograd on the morning of 25 October and tried to raise troops from the front, while the rest of the government remained in the Winter Palace. He could secure no further help. The troops guarding the Provisional Government – the Women's Battalion (known as the Amazons) and the military cadets – surrendered. When the cruiser *Aurora* sailed up the River Neva and fired its guns, the Provisional Government gave in and was placed under arrest. Some of its members were able to slip away unnoticed. In all, the actions of the day had ended with the death of six soldiers, eighteen arrests and the collapse of the Provisional Government.

▲ **Source D** Bolsheviks outside the Smolny Institute, October 1917

The Bolsheviks take power

Meanwhile, the All-Russian Congress of Soviets was assembling at the Smolny Institute. The Bolsheviks held the most seats – 390 of 650. The SR (see page 12) and Menshevik representatives condemned the Bolshevik actions, because it was not a **Soviet** takeover of power. The two sets of representatives left the Congress which meant that the Bolsheviks' position was strengthened because of their huge majority.

The following day, Lenin formed a government called the **Council of People's Commissars**. This had an all-Bolshevik membership:

- Lenin was the head of the government
- Leon Trotsky (see page 35) was **Commissar** of Foreign Affairs
- Joseph Stalin (see page 72) was Commissar for Nationalities.

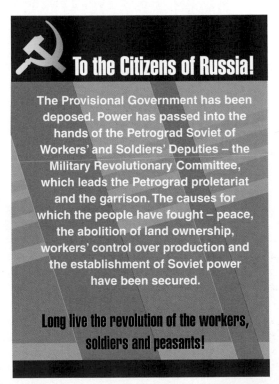

▲ **Source E** An artist's interpretation of a poster, dated 5 November 1917, written by Lenin, announcing that the Bolsheviks had removed the Provisional Government

> **ACTIVITY** ?
>
> Study Source E. Why was Lenin careful to address the poster to 'workers, soldiers and peasants'?

> **Practice question**
>
> Give two things you can infer from Source C about Lenin's role in the Bolshevik Revolution. (*For guidance, see page 77.*)

4.3 Different interpretations of the Bolshevik Revolution

In the years following the Bolshevik takeover historians in the Soviet Union claimed that the takeover was a popular uprising which was led and carried out by the **working class**, supported by the poorer peasants. This interpretation stressed the key role played by the Bolshevik Party, especially Lenin, in guiding the working classes and making the crucial decisions about the timing and organisation of the revolution. Certainly leading Bolsheviks such as Lenin and Trotsky did play a crucial role in the takeover. However, other interpretations suggest that it was a takeover by a small minority rather than a popular revolution. For example, in the November elections for the Constituent Assembly that followed the revolution (see page 41) the Bolsheviks got fewer than a quarter of the seats. Even though membership of the party had grown since the return of Lenin, it was still only 340,000 out of a total Russian population of about 125 million.

The storming of the Winter Palace

There are also different interpretations of the storming of the Winter Palace on 25 October. According to the Bolsheviks, **Red Guards**, supported by the masses, heroically stormed the Winter Palace, broke in and arrested the ministers. In later years this event was celebrated in pictures, mainly painted in the 1930s (see Source F), as well as Eisenstein's film *October: Ten Days that Shook the World,* released in 1928.

In fact, the story was quite different. Bolshevik Red Guards, soldiers and sailors arrived in the square in front of the Winter Palace around noon on 25 October. The palace was defended by cadets from a military school, 200 members of the Women's Death Battalion and two divisions of **Cossacks**, grumbling about having to fight alongside 'women with guns'. Due to Bolshevik inefficiency, no attack took place in the afternoon. By early evening many of the soldiers in the palace had panicked and fled. After the cruiser *Aurora* fired its shell to signal the beginning of the attack, the Women's Battalion was allowed to leave the Palace unharmed. In the next few hours, Bolshevik soldiers filtered into the palace by various entrances and wandered the corridors disarming the few remaining cadets, who put up little resistance. Eventually a group forced their way into the room where the last members of the Provisional Government were assembled and arrested them. This was the so-called heroic storming of the Winter Palace!

ACTIVITY ?

Study Source F. Devise a suitable Soviet caption for this painting to fit in with the Bolshevik interpretation of the revolution.

◀ **Source F** A painting by a Soviet artist in 1939 showing the Storming of the Winter Palace on 25th October, 1917

4.4 Reasons for the success of the Bolshevik takeover

Both Trotsky and Lenin played important roles in the success of the **Bolshevik Revolution**. There were other reasons for its success as well, namely the weaknesses of the Provisional Government and the lack of alternatives to it.

The role Trotsky

As you can see from his biographical details (see box), Trotsky was a Menshevik exile at the time of the February Revolution. On his return to Russia in May 1917, he was concerned that many **Mensheviks** were supporting the Provisional Government. He was arrested in July as a result of his revolutionary activities and the following month he became an official Bolshevik Party member.

When the Bolsheviks secured control of the Petrograd Soviet, Trotsky was elected as its leader and this became the key to his success. In October, he became the dominant member of the three-man **Military Revolutionary Committee (MRC)** of the Soviet. This provided a useful screen for his secret preparations. The MRC – in theory – controlled 20,000 Red Guards, 60,000 Baltic sailors and the 150,000 soldiers of the Petrograd garrison.

In October, the Bolsheviks began to reduce their massive demonstrations and street skirmishes, because the crowds were not always easy to control. When they started preparing for the revolution, they began to rely more on small, disciplined units of soldiers and workers. From his office in the Smolny Institute, a building formerly used as a girls' school, Trotsky made his plans for the seizure of the key buildings of the Provisional Government and the overthrow of the Provisional Government on 24 October (see Sources H and J).

Source G From *Memoirs of a Revolutionary* by Victor Serge. Serge was a Bolshevik, writing in 1945 about Trotsky

I first saw Trotsky at a packed meeting of the Petrograd Soviet. He was all tension and energy. He outshone Lenin through his oratorical talent, his organising ability, first with the army and then with the railways, and by his brilliant gift as a student of political theory.

Source H From *History of the Russian Revolution*, written by Trotsky in 1932. He was describing his time in the Smolny Institute during October 1917

The Smolny Institute was being transformed into a fortress. In the top floor there were about two dozen machine-guns. All the reports about the movements of troops, the attitude of soldiers and workers, the agitation in the barracks, the happenings in the Winter Palace – all these came to the Smolny.

LEON TROTSKY, 1879–1940

1879	Born Lev Davidovich Bronstein
1897	Involved in organising the South Russian Workers' Union
1898	Arrested and spent four years in exile in Siberia
1902	Escaped and fled to London, assuming the name Trotsky. Joined the Social Democratic (SD) Party
1903	Followed Martov and became a Menshevik
1905	Returned to St Petersburg and was eventually elected Chairman of the Soviet. Arrested and imprisoned
1906	Exiled to Siberia but escaped after two years
1914	Moved to Zürich and then Paris, where he denounced the war and encouraged workers not to fight
1916	Deported to Spain and then went to the USA
1917 May	Returned to Russia in May. Chairman of Petrograd Soviet in September and member of Military Revolutionary Committee (MRC). Commissar for Foreign Affairs
1918	Commissar for War

Source I From a speech by Trotsky to the Petrograd Soviet, 22 October 1917

The Soviet government will give everything the country has to the poor and to the soldiers at the front ... We will defend the cause of the workers and peasants to the last drop of blood.

Source J From an article by Joseph Stalin in *Pravda*, 6 November 1918

All the work of practical organisation of the revolution was conducted under the immediate leadership of the Chairman of the Petrograd Soviet, Trotsky. It is possible to declare with certainty that the swift passing of the garrison to the side of the Soviet and the bold execution of the Military Revolutionary Committee, the Party owes principally and above all to Comrade Trotsky.

ACTIVITIES

1 What can you learn about Trotsky's character from Source G?
2 What do Sources H and J suggest about Trotsky's role in the Bolshevik takeover?

The role of Lenin

The role of Lenin in the success of the revolution was crucial. Lenin persuaded the Bolsheviks to oppose the war, unlike the Mensheviks and Socialist Revolutionaries. These two parties were still following Marx's ideas that the workers' revolution was many years away – Lenin had already changed his views in the April Theses (see page 31). He gave the Bolsheviks simple slogans which were easily understood by the ordinary people and designed to gain their support, such as 'Peace, Bread, Land' and 'All power to the soviets'.

Lenin had tremendous energy and vitality and his commitment to revolution spurred on the Bolsheviks. His decision to oppose the war was the key reason why Bolshevik support rose throughout 1917 (see page 30). He created the Red Guard which was funded by German money which helped to equip them. Lenin persuaded the majority of the **Central Committee** of the Bolshevik Party to seize power in October. Trotsky organised the takeover, but without Lenin the Bolsheviks would not have even tried to remove the Provisional Government. Within a week of the revolution in Petrograd, the Bolsheviks took control of Moscow and then began the work of securing control of the whole of Russia.

▲ **Source K** A cartoon showing Lenin sweeping away his opponents. The caption reads 'Lenin cleans the earth of evil spirits'

Practice question

How useful are Sources I and J (see page 35) for an enquiry into the role of Trotsky in organising the Bolshevik Revolution? Explain your answer, using Sources I and J and your knowledge of the historical context. (*For guidance, see pages 85–87*.)

VLADIMIR ILLICH ULYANOV (ASSUMED NAME LENIN) 1870–1924

Key events to 1917

1870	Born Vladimir Illich Ulyanov
1887	Elder brother, Alexander, hanged as a conspirator in the attempted assassination of Tsar Alexander III
1897	Exiled to Siberia – adopted the name Lenin
1898	Married Nadezhda Krupskaya
1902	Wrote 'What is to be done?' in which he put forward the central role of dedicated party members in any revolution
1903	Led the Bolsheviks in the Social Democrat Party split (see page 12)
1906	Exiled for much of the next 11 years
1912	Secured control of the Central Committee (the body responsible for making policies)
1917 April	Returned to Russia – set out Bolshevik plans in the 'April Theses'
1917 July	Tried to overthrow the Provisional Government in the 'July Days'. Lenin fled to Finland to avoid arrest
1917 October	Returned to Russia and led the Bolshevik Revolution

ACTIVITIES ?

1 a) Read this page on Lenin's role in the Bolshevik Revolution and also pages 30–31 about his return in April 1917 and the following months. Construct a concept map of his contribution to the Bolshevik Revolution.
   b) Using the information and sources on page 35, explain Trotsky's role in preparing the Bolsheviks for revolution.
   c) Using the information and sources on page 27–29, explain the role of Kerensky in the downfall of the Provisional Government and the success of the Bolshevik takeover.
   d) Using your work in activities a)–c), make a judgement on whether Lenin, Trotsky or Kerensky's role was more significant in the success of the Bolshevik Revolution. Explain your judgement.

2 Study Source K. Which groups in society are being swept away by Lenin?

Other reasons for the Bolshevik's success

There were, however, other important reasons for the Bolshevik success.

The weaknesses of the Provisional Government

The Provisional Government was weak and really only a temporary body. The people of Russia had not elected it. Moreover, from the beginning, it shared power in Petrograd with the Soviet and could not overturn Soviet Order Number One (see page 25).

Kerensky was never able to remove the Bolsheviks completely and during the Kornilov Revolt he actually armed them (see page 28). As 1917 unfolded, the Provisional Government was unable to win over the support of ordinary people in Petrograd – the Bolsheviks and other parties were able to publish so much propaganda that when the crisis came in October, Kerensky received little or no help (see Interpretation 2).

> **Interpretation 2** An extract from *Reaction and Revolution* by Michael Lynch, published in 1992
>
> The failure of the Provisional Government to rally effective military support in its hour of need was symptomatic of its much deeper failure over the previous eight months ... Kerensky's government came nowhere near to solving Russia's problems or satisfying her needs. Hence its support evaporated ... militarily disastrous, the Provisional Government was not considered to be worth struggling to save.

Bolshevik control of the armed forces

Trotsky claimed that the Bolsheviks were successful because the soldiers of the Petrograd garrison did not side with the Provisional Government. Furthermore, the creation of the Military Revolutionary Committee enabled the Bolsheviks to control some of the armed forces at a critical time.

Lack of alternatives

The many political parties did not offer clear leadership during 1917. They all became discredited because they supported the continuation of the war. This led to discontent within the army. The elections to the Constituent Assembly were delayed and the peasants' demand for land was not addressed. Consequently, anarchy and the seizing of land in the countryside increased as 1917 wore on, and **left-wing** agitators infiltrated the army and destroyed the morale of the soldiers.

ACTIVITIES ?

1 What can you learn from Interpretation 2 about Kerensky and the Provisional Government in late 1917?

2 Working in small groups, choose one of the following statements and prepare a case for class discussion. Ensure that you use the sources and information from this chapter and also Chapter 3.
   - Lenin was the key to Bolshevik success.
   - Trotsky was the key to Bolshevik success.
   - The mistakes of the Provisional Government were the key to Bolshevik success.

3 Working in pairs produce a timeline to help you understand the key events and developments of 1917 (you will also need to refer to Chapters 2 and 3).

Practice question

Explain why the Bolshevik takeover of October 1917 was successful.

> You may use the following in your answer.
> - The weaknesses of the Provisional Government
> - The role of Trotsky
>
> You must also use information of your own.

(For guidance, see page 95–96.)

4.5 How interpretations differ

This section provides guidance on how to answer the question in the exam that asks how two interpretations differ.

Question

Study Interpretations 1 and 2. They give different views about the events of the Bolshevik Revolution. What is the main difference between the views? Explain your answer, using details from both interpretations.

Interpretation 1 From *History of the USSR,* by Y. Kukushkin, a Soviet historian, published in 1981. He is describing the attack on the Winter Palace

The signal for the start of the assault was given from the cruiser 'Aurora' which fired a blank shot from her gun. The Red Guards, sailors and soldiers poured from the adjacent streets in an irresistible rush across the square in front of the Winter Palace. The last remnants of the forces that opposed the revolution fell on the night of 25–26 October, 1917. This marked a victory of the armed uprising of the working people in the capital of Russia, Petrograd which began a new era in human history.

Interpretation 2 From *A People's Tragedy: The Russian Revolution 1891–1924* by. O. Figes, published in 1997

The great October Socialist Revolution was in reality such a small-scale event that it passed unnoticed by the majority of the inhabitants of Petrograd. The legendary storming of the Winter Palace was more like a routine house arrest, since most of the force defending the palace had already left for home, hungry and dejected, before the final attack began. Trotsky himself claimed that 25,000 to 30,000 'at the most' were actively involved – about 5 per cent of the workers and soldiers in the city.

How to answer

You are being asked to explain the main difference in the views each interpretation has about the events of the Bolshevik Revolution of October 1917.

Step 1
You will need to identify the main view that Interpretation 1 has about the events of the Bolshevik Revolution.

Example
Interpretation 1 suggests that the Bolshevik Revolution was a popular revolution achieved by a mass attack on the Winter Palace.

Step 2
You will need evidence from Interpretation 1 to support this view.

Example
I know this because the interpretation says that sailors and soldiers made an irresistible rush to the Winter Palace and the Bolshevik Revolution marked a victory of the working people in the capital of Russia, Petrograd.

Step 3
You will need to identify the main view that Interpretation 2 has about the events of the Bolshevik Revolution. Use the phrase 'on the other hand' to show that this interpretation gives a different view.

Example
On the other hand, Interpretation 2 suggests that there was not a mass storming of the Winter Palace and a popular revolution.

Step 4
You will need evidence from Interpretation 2 to support this view.

Example
I know this because the interpretation says that the legendary storming of the Winter Palace was more like a house arrest and only 25,000 to 30,000 took part in the revolution.

Try explaining the main difference between the views in your own words.

The Bolsheviks in power, 1917–24

This key topic examines the key developments in Russia between 1917 and 1924. In the early years the Bolsheviks were able to consolidate their position in power through the removal of opposition, the execution of Nicholas II and his family and the defeat of the Whites in the Civil War of 1918–21. Moreover, the Bolsheviks brought in a series of policies which brought about significant economic and social changes before Lenin's death in 1924

Each chapter within this key topic explains a key issue and examines important lines of enquiry, as outlined in the boxes below. There will also be guidance on how to answer the interpretations question:

- How to answer the second question on interpretations, suggesting one reason why they give different views (pages 46–47).
- How to answer the third question on interpretations: how far do you agree with one of the interpretations? (pages 55–56).

CHAPTER 5 EARLY CONSOLIDATION OF POWER, 1917–18

- The early Bolshevik decrees of November–December 1917.
- The removal of opposition, including the Constituent Assembly and the execution of Tsar Nicholas II and his family.
- The reasons for, the main terms and the significance of the Treaty of Brest-Litovsk and different reactions in Russia to the Treaty.

CHAPTER 6 THE CIVIL WAR, 1918–21

- The reasons for, key events and effects of the Civil War.
- The reasons for the Bolshevik victory, including the strengths of the Bolsheviks, role of Trotsky, foreign intervention and the weaknesses of the Whites.

CHAPTER 7 CHANGES UNDER THE BOLSHEVIKS, 1918–24

- The Red Terror and the role of the *Cheka*.
- Bolshevik centralisation including the role of Lenin and the Politburo. The setting up of the USSR.
- Reasons for and features of War Communism and reasons for its unpopularity.
- Reasons for and features of the New Economic Policy. The different reactions to it and its effects on the economy from 1921–24.
- Social changes, including the impact of Bolshevik policies on women, education and culture.

TIMELINE

1917 November–December	Bolsheviks issue a series of decrees
1917 November	Elections for the Constituent Assembly
1917 December	*Cheka* created
1918 January	Constituent Assembly dissolved. Red Army created
1918 March	Treaty of Brest-Litovsk
1918 April	Start of Russian Civil War
1918 July	Introduction of War Communism. Execution of the tsar and his family
1918 September	Red Terror officially introduced
1921	End of Civil War – Bolshevik victory
1921 March	Kronstadt Mutiny
1921	Ending of War Communism. Introduction of the New Economic Policy (NEP)
1922	Russia became the Union of Soviet Socialist Republics (USSR)
1924	Death of Lenin

The Bolsheviks had seized power with hardly any bloodshed. The Provisional Government melted away and Lenin was left to set up a government. However, the Bolsheviks did not have widespread support across Russia and Lenin was keen to impose his control on the country as soon as was feasible. The Bolsheviks introduced a series of decrees in order to increase their support, especially among the industrial workers and the peasants, and ended the war with Germany by agreeing to sign the Treaty of Brest-Litovsk.

5.1 Early Bolshevik decrees

The government that Lenin set up in November 1917 was called *Sovnarkom*, short for **Council of People's Commissars**. During the weeks after the **Bolshevik** takeover, **soviets** throughout Russia joined in the **revolution** and took control of most towns and cities. By the end of 1917, nearly all Russia was in soviet hands. However, this did not mean that Lenin and the Bolsheviks had total control of Russia, since not all the soviets were run by Bolsheviks. In the countryside, most peasants supported the Socialist Revolutionaries.

Even more awkward from Lenin's point of view, in the upcoming elections to the **Constituent Assembly** (a new parliament) that the **Provisional Government** had arranged before the Revolution, it seemed that the Socialist Revolutionaries would win more votes than the Bolsheviks. If that happened, the Bolsheviks would have to hand over control of *Sovnarkom* to their rivals.

On top of these problems, Lenin had to keep promises he had openly made in his April Theses (see page 31), such as giving land to the peasants. To address this, *Sovnarkom*, with Lenin as chairman, issued a series of decrees in November and December 1917 (see Tables 5.1 and 5.2 opposite).

ACTIVITIES ?

1 Describe two problems Lenin faced when the Bolsheviks first took over in 1917.
2 Look at the November and December decrees in Tables 5.1 and 5.2. Create a table and fill it in to explain why each section in Russian society listed below would support or oppose the decrees.
    - Worker
    - Peasant
    - Middle classes
    - Nobility
3 Working in pairs, look at the decrees passed by the Bolsheviks in November and December 1917 and discuss the following questions:
    a) Did Lenin follow the April Theses (see page 31)?
    b) In what ways might some people say that Lenin ruled like the tsar?

▼ **Table 5.1** November decrees

Decree	Description
Decree on land	540 million acres of land taken from the tsar, the nobles, the Church and other landlords. Peasants to set up committees to divide the land fairly.
Decree on unemployment insurance	Employment insurance to be introduced for all workers against injury, illness and unemployment.
Decree on peace	*Sovnarkom* intended to make peace immediately with Russia's opponents in the war.
Decree on work	Introduction of an 8-hour day and 40-hour week for all industrial workers. There were restrictions on overtime and there was to be holiday entitlement for workers.
Decree on titles	All titles and class distinctions were abolished. Women were declared equal to men.
Decree on the press	All non-Bolshevik newspapers were banned.

▼ **Table 5.2** December Decrees

Decree	Description
Decree on workers' control	All factories to be placed under the control of elected committees of workers.
Decree to set up the political police	The 'All Russian Extraordinary Commission to fight **Counter-Revolution** and Espionage' was formed, known as the *Cheka*.
Decree on political parties	Russia's main liberal party, the Constitutional Democratic Party, was banned.
Decree on banking	All banks in Russia came under *Sovnarkom*'s control.
Decree on marriage	Couples could have non-religious weddings and divorce was made easier.

5.2 The Constituent Assembly

Elections were held for Russia's new parliament, the Constituent Assembly, in November 1917. They were the first free elections in Russian history. The Socialist Revolutionaries (SRs) gained more seats in the Assembly than all the other parties put together (see Table 5.3).

▼ **Table 5.3** Number of seats of different parties in the Constituent Assembly, 1917. Total number of seats = 707

Party	Number of seats
Socialist Revolutionaries	370
Bolsheviks	175
Others (representing subject nationalities)	87
Left-wing Socialist Revolutionaries	40
Constitutional Democrats (Cadets)	17
Mensheviks	16
Narodniks	2

Lenin was concerned that the Bolsheviks had gained only a quarter of the votes and these were primarily from the **working classes** of the cities. He was also concerned that some of the nationalities, such as Finns and Estonians, were trying to break away and he wanted to avoid the disintegration of Russia.

Lenin wrote an article for *Pravda*, the Bolshevik newspaper, in which he stated that, because there were soviets in Russia, there was no need for the Constituent Assembly.

Nevertheless, the Constituent Assembly met on 18 January 1918. It had the job of drawing up a new **constitution** for Russia. The Bolsheviks and the left-wing SRs proposed that the power of the Assembly be limited. When this proposal was defeated, Lenin made his decision to dissolve the Assembly.

Fewer than 24 hours after the Constituent Assembly had met, Lenin gave the order to dissolve it. Bolshevik **Red Guards** killed and wounded more than 100 people who demonstrated outside the Tauride Palace in support of the Assembly. Two leaders of the Cadets were killed in a hospital. The Red Guards then prevented the elected Deputies from entering the Assembly and closed it down permanently. Lenin had removed a threat to the Bolsheviks and *Sovnarkom* at a stroke.

Practice question

How useful are Sources B and C for an enquiry into Lenin's dissolution of the Constituent Assembly in January 1918? Explain your answer using Sources B and C and your knowledge of the historical context. (*For guidance, see pages 85–87.*)

Source A From a newspaper article written in 1948 by Victor Chernov, leader of the Socialist Revolutionary Party in 1918

When we, the newly elected members of the Constituent Assembly, met on 18 January 1918, we found that the corridors were full of armed guards. Every sentence of my speech was met with outcries, some ironical, others accompanied by the waving of guns. Lenin lounged in his chair with the air of a man who was bored to death.

Source B From the memoirs of Edgar Sissons, written in 1931. Sissons was the US Special Representative in Russia in 1918

The Constituent Assembly met in a ring of steel. Armed guards were all about us ... a line of guards stood or walked in the connecting corridor, and at every door was a pair of sailors or soldiers. Even the ushers were armed men.

Source C From an interview with C. Lindhagen, a Swedish eyewitness at the opening of the Constituent Assembly

In one of the corridors a group of armed soldiers could be glimpsed. I was informed that several of the Deputies (members) as well as the commissars were armed. I asked one of the commissars whether this was true. 'Of course' and he showed me the butt of a revolver in his pocket.

ACTIVITIES

1 What do the election results (Table 5.3) suggest about the political situation in Russia at the beginning of 1918?

2 How could Lenin justify dissolving the Constituent Assembly? Write a speech in which Lenin explains to the Bolshevik Party why he must dissolve the Constituent Assembly.

3 By January 1918, why were some Russians beginning to compare Lenin, unfavourably, with the tsar? Explain your answer carefully.

4 What similarities and differences are there between Sources A, B and C in their views about the dissolution of the Constituent Assembly? To help you answer this, plan your answer using a copy of the grid below.

	A–B	B–C	A–C
Similarities			
Differences			

5.3 The execution of Tsar Nicholas II and his family

On 19 July 1918, a Bolshevik newspaper announced the death of Nicholas II and that the 'wife and son of Nicholas Romanov have been sent to a safe place'. In fact, all the royal family had been murdered, but the Bolsheviks were afraid to acknowledge that they had done this in case it lost them public sympathy. They also didn't want to upset the Germans, because Alexandra, the tsar's wife, was German.

The tsar and his family 1917–18

After his abdication in February 1917, the tsar and his family had been allowed to live in the royal palace at Tsarskoye Selo. However, this was close to Petrograd and the Provisional Government were afraid that the royal family was so unpopular that they would be attacked by local people. Therefore, they were moved to Tobolsk in Siberia.

In April 1918, as the White armies gained control of Siberia in the Civil War (see box), the Bolsheviks moved them to Ekaterinburg in the Ural Mountains. They were met at the station by an angry mob and imprisoned in a large white house which belonged to a retired businessman.

Reasons for the execution

Right until the collapse of communism in Russia in the late twentieth century, the Soviet authorities insisted that the murder was carried out by the local Bolsheviks in Ekaterinburg who feared that the Romanovs would fall into the hands of the advancing White armies.

However, the opening up of the Soviet archives in the 1990s, showed that, in fact, the decision was taken by Lenin in the first week of July 1918 because of advice given to him by Goloshchekin, a leading Bolshevik. Goloshchekin was sent to Ekaterinburg to organise the execution and sent a coded telegram to Lenin on 16 July, informing him that the execution had to take place because the Czech Legion (see page 49) was surrounding the city. The local Bolsheviks had only a few hundred Red Guards and little chance of safely evacuating the Romanovs. There was every chance that the royal family would be handed over to the Whites and provide an even greater focal point for the opponents of the Bolsheviks. Indeed, the city fell to Czechs, eight days after the murder.

> **Source D** From an entry in Trotsky's diary of 1935 in which he recalls a conversation with Sverdlov, a leading Bolshevik, shortly after the murder
>
> Speaking with Sverdlov, I asked in passing, 'Oh, yes, where is the tsar?' 'Finished', he replied. 'He has been shot'. 'And where is the family?' 'The family has been shot along with him'. 'All?', I asked. 'All', Sverdlov replied. 'And who decided the matter', I enquired. 'We decided it here. Illich [Lenin] thought that we should not leave the Whites a live banner, especially under the present difficult circumstances'.

RUSSIAN CIVIL WAR, 1918–21

The Russian Civil War lasted for almost three years and involved many groups. The Bolsheviks faced threats from various armies, Including the White armies of Russian Generals, the Czech Legion and foreign powers such as the British and French. You will learn more about the Civil War on pages 48–54.

The execution

On 4 July the local Cheka (Bolshevik secret police), led by Yakov Yurovsky, took over the responsibility of guarding the Romanovs and carrying out the execution. At 2 a.m. on 17 July, Nicholas and his family were led into the basement of the house. None of them seemed aware of what was about to happen. They had been told that there had been shooting in the street and it was safer for them to be in the basement.

Yurovsky entered the room with the murder squad – six Hungarians. He read out the order to shoot the Romanovs. Nicholas asked him to repeat the order and his last words were 'What? What?' Yurovsky shot Nicholas at point blank range. Nicholas and his wife died instantly. Despite firing many shots, Alexis and Anastasia still showed signs of life. Alexis was finished off by two shots from Yurovsky and Anastasia was bayoneted several times.

After the murder, the bodies were driven off in a lorry and buried in the ground. Sulphuric acid was poured on their faces to hide the identity of the corpses should they be discovered. News of the execution reached Lenin the following day. The real significance of the murder was that it was a declaration of terror. It was a statement that from now on individuals would count for nothing in the Civil War.

◄ **Source E** A painting by Sarmet, a White supporter, showing the murder of the Romanovs. It was painted in 1923 and based on a White investigation into the assassination

Practice questions

1 Give two things you can infer from Source D about the death of the tsar. (*For guidance, see page 77.*)

2 How useful are Sources D and E for an enquiry into the execution of Tsar Nicholas II and his family? Explain your answer, using Sources D and E and your knowledge of the historical context. (*For guidance, see page 85–87.*)

5.4 The Treaty of Brest-Litovsk

In March 1918, the Bolsheviks signed the Treaty of Brest-Litovsk with Germany, formally ending Russian involvement in the First World War.

Reasons for the Treaty

Lenin had opposed the war against Germany from the very beginning, and much of the support the Bolsheviks had gained came from their opposition to the conflict. He was aware that if the Bolsheviks were to hold onto the power they had won in October 1917, then there would have to be an immediate peace settlement. His greatest concern was that any prolongation of the war would mean that the army would not continue to support him. *Sovnarkom* issued a Decree on Peace in November to show the intention to end the war (see Source F).

> **Source F** Decree on Peace, issued by *Sovnarkom* in November 1917
>
> The workers' and peasants' government proposes to all the warring peoples and their governments that they enter immediately into talks for a just peace. This sort of peace would be an immediate one without seizure of foreign territory and without financial penalties.

Peace talks with Germany began on 3 December 1917 and Lenin sent Trotsky (**Commissar** for Foreign Affairs) as Russia's representative. Talks were held at Brest-Litovsk, near the German border. Trotsky and his negotiating team tried to prolong the talks as long as possible, because they believed that workers in central Europe were on the brink of revolution. When this revolution came, the war would end and then Germany and Russia would make a fair peace.

Terms of the Treaty

As the German army advanced into Russia in February 1918 (see Source H), Lenin's hand was forced and he decided to make peace (see Source G). The terms of the treaty were the harshest possible. Russia had to surrender huge tracts of land from the Black Sea to the Baltic (see Figure 5.1). In addition, Russia had to pay reparations amounting to 3 billion roubles. The impact on Russia's economy would be immense.

> **Source G** Lenin speaking in March 1918 about the Treaty of Brest-Litovsk
>
> Our impulse tells us to refuse to sign this robber peace ... Russia can offer no physical resistance because she is materially exhausted by three years of war ... The Russian Revolution must sign the peace to obtain a breathing space to recuperate for the struggle.

▼ **Source H** German troops with the heaped-up bodies of dead Russian soldiers, early 1918

Reactions in Russia to the Treaty

Patriotic Russians were horrified by the terms. Giving away large chunks of Russian homeland antagonised many Russians, irrespective of class or party, and encouraged them to join anti-Bolshevik groups. They objected to the Treaty for the following reasons:

- The dictated nature of the peace.
- The way in which Lenin and Trotsky were prepared to sacrifice national interest to secure peace at almost any price.
- The amount of land and population lost.
- The amount of reparations.

Moreover, Lenin was heavily criticised by many Bolsheviks for accepting the Treaty. Bukharin, a leading Bolshevik and editor of *Pravda*, and the left-wing of the party saw it as a shameful peace, which helped Germany to survive as an imperial power. However, Lenin won the debate in the **Central Committee** of the Bolshevik Party about the Treaty, but only by the narrowest of margins.

Significance of the Treaty

Lenin's decision to make peace was a huge gamble, because he made it on the assumption that ultimately Germany would be defeated in the war, although this was by no means certain in March 1918. Nevertheless, Lenin's gamble paid off. With the arrival of US troops on the **Western Front** and the failure of the **German Spring Offensive**, war in Europe was over in the autumn of 1918 and the Treaty of Brest-Litovsk became meaningless. The defeat of Germany now meant that the Treaty had no legality. However, the Treaty was significant, as peace had given Lenin and his government valuable breathing space to consolidate itself. Yet, just as the major danger of Germany was removed, Lenin had to face serious internal threats and, by the spring of 1918, Russia was convulsed by civil war.

▼ **Figure 5.1** Territory lost by Russia at the Treaty of Brest-Litovsk. Key population centres, coal mining and iron production areas were in the west

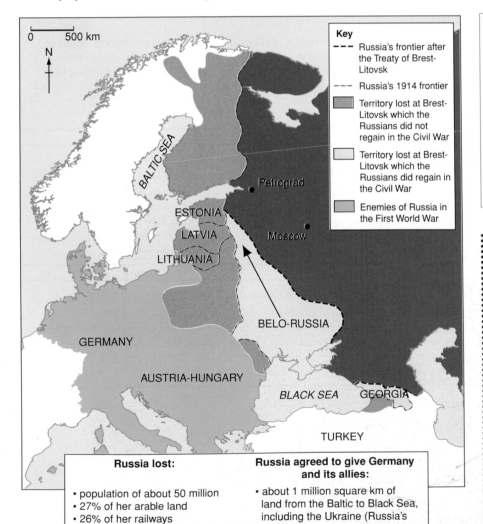

Key
- - - Russia's frontier after the Treaty of Brest-Litovsk
- - - Russia's 1914 frontier

Territory lost at Brest-Litovsk which the Russians did not regain in the Civil War

Territory lost at Brest-Litovsk which the Russians did regain in the Civil War

Enemies of Russia in the First World War

Russia lost:	Russia agreed to give Germany and its allies:
• population of about 50 million • 27% of her arable land • 26% of her railways • 74% of her iron and coal	• about 1 million square km of land from the Baltic to Black Sea, including the Ukraine (Russia's main grain source) • war damage of 3 billion roubles

ACTIVITIES

1 Study Sources G and H and the information on these pages. Explain why Lenin was keen to make a peace settlement with Germany.

2 Study the material on these two pages and use your own knowledge about Russia's involvement in the war to list the reasons why Lenin faced opposition to signing the Treaty of Brest-Litovsk.

Practice questions

1 Give two things you can infer from Source G about the reasons for the Treaty of Brest-Litovsk. (*For guidance, see page 77.*)

2 Explain why the Bolshevik were able to consolidate their power from November 1917 to March 1918.

You may use the following in your answer:
- The Constituent Assembly
- The Treaty of Brest-Litovsk

You must also use information of your own.

(*For guidance, see pages 95–96.*)

5.5 Why the interpretations differ

This section provides guidance on how to answer the question which asks you to suggest one reason why the interpretations give different views. Look at the question below. Then read the guidance on how to answer it on page 47.

Question

Suggest one reason why Interpretations 1 and 2 give different views about the Bolshevik Revolution of October 1917. You may use Sources A and B to help explain your answer.

> **Interpretation 1** From *History of the USSR,* by Y. Kukushkin, a Soviet historian, published in 1981. He is describing the attack on the Winter Palace
>
> The signal for the start of the assault was given from the cruiser 'Aurora' which fired a blank shot from her gun. The Red Guards, sailors and soldiers poured from the adjacent streets in an irresistible rush across the square in front of the Winter Palace. The last remnants of the forces that opposed the revolution fell on the night of 25–26 October, 1917. This marked a victory of the armed uprising of the working people in the capital of Russia, Petrograd which began a new era in human history.

> **Interpretation 2** From *A People's Tragedy: The Russian Revolution 1891–1924* by O. Figes, published in 1997
>
> The great October Socialist Revolution was in reality such a small-scale event that it passed unnoticed by the majority of the inhabitants of Petrograd. The legendary storming of the Winter Palace was more like a routine house arrest, since most of the force defending the palace had already left for home, hungry and dejected, before the final attack began. Trotsky himself claimed that 25,000 to 30,000 'at the most' were actively involved – about 5 per cent of the workers and soldiers in the city.

> **Source A** From P. Sorokin, a Socialist Revolutionary, describing the Bolshevik attack on the Provisional Government on 25 October 1917
>
> I learned that the Bolsheviks had brought up the warship Aurora and had opened fire on the Winter Palace, demanding the surrender of the members of the Provisional Government still barricaded there … There was a regiment of women and young military trainees bravely resisting an overwhelming force of Bolshevik troops … Poor women, poor lads, their situation was desperate, for we knew the wild sailors would tear them to pieces.

> **Source B** From Sukhanov, a Menshevik, describing the Bolshevik takeover of Petrograd
>
> No resistance was shown. Beginning at two in the morning the stations, bridges and telegraphs were gradually occupied by small forces brought from the barracks. The little group of cadets could not resist and did not think of it. In general, the military operations in the politically important cities resembled the changing of the guard. The decisive operations were quite bloodless. The city was absolutely calm.

How to answer

On page 38 you were shown how to explain one difference between these two interpretations. Now you have to give one reason why these interpretations are different. You can use the sources to help you with this answer.

There are three reasons as to why the two interpretations differ. You will only need to give one of these.

First possible reason (remember you only have to explain one of the reasons).

The interpretations may differ because they have given weight to two different sources. You need to identify the views given in the two sources.

Example

Source A suggests that it was a mass attack on the Winter Palace by a very large Bolshevik force. Source B suggests that the Bolsheviks were only a small force who faced no resistance and easily took over the key buildings.

Now you need to show how the sources match the views of the two interpretations and identify the views given in the interpretations that match.

Example

Source A provides some support for Interpretation 1 which stresses that the takeover was achieved by a large force of Bolsheviks with popular support. Source B provides some support for Interpretation 2 which suggests that the revolution was achieved by a small number of Bolsheviks who faced very little opposition.

Second possible reason (remember you only have to explain one of the reasons).

The interpretations may differ because they are partial extracts and, in this case, they do not actually contradict one another. Remember to make reference to the views given in each interpretation.

Example

Both interpretations suggest that the success of the Bolshevik takeover was because the Bolsheviks faced very little opposition, with Interpretation 1 describing them as the last remnants of the forces that opposed the revolution and Interpretation 2 explaining that most of the forces defending the palace had left for home, hungry and dejected, before the final attack.

Third possible reason (remember you only have to explain one of the reasons).

They may differ because the authors have a different emphasis.

Example

Interpretation 1 focuses more on the achievements of the Bolsheviks during the October Revolution, especially their success in capturing the Winter Palace, and stresses the apparent mass support from the working classes. On the other hand, Interpretation 2 focuses more on the lack of opposition to the Bolsheviks in the Winter Palace and the limited numbers who took part in the revolution.

6 The Civil War, 1918–21

The Russian Civil War lasted for almost three years and involved many groups. Furthermore, it was complicated by the involvement of foreign countries, many of which had been Russia's allies in the First World War. The Civil War seemed to bring together all the problems of the tsarist years, the First World War and the revolutions of 1917. Nevertheless, the Bolsheviks were eventually successful due to their own strengths, more especially the military leadership of Trotsky, as well as the weaknesses of their opponents, the Whites, and in particular their disunity.

6.1 Reasons for the Civil War

The **Bolsheviks** faced opposition from a variety of groups following their takeover in October 1917. This culminated in a civil war, lasting from 1918 to 1921. One of the main reasons for opposition was economic and social hardship, but there was also opposition to the reforms the Bolsheviks had introduced, to their dissolution of the **Constituent Assembly**, and to the signing of the Treaty of Brest-Litovsk.

Economic and social hardship

In the six months following the October Revolution, the Bolsheviks had failed to deal with the country's most pressing need – food shortages and starvation – especially in the towns and cities (see Sources A and B). This was an important reason for the growth of opposition to the Bolsheviks. In March 1918, the bread ration in Petrograd reached its lowest ever allocation of 50 grams per day. Hunger drove many industrial workers out of the major industrial cities in search of food. By June 1918, the workforce in Petrograd had shrunk by 60 per cent and the overall population had declined by between 2 and 3 million.

These dire circumstances in the towns and cities led to growing violence and encouraged open challenges to the Bolsheviks.

> **Source A** An eyewitness account by a British refugee from Petrograd in 1918, who is writing to his family in England
>
> It is a common occurrence when a horse falls down in the street for the people to cut off the flesh of the animal the moment it has breathed its last. Another way of getting food is by buying it at excessive prices from members of the Red Guard who are well fed.

> **Source B** From *Memoirs of a Revolutionary* by V. Serge, 1945. Serge became a Bolshevik in 1919 but left the party in 1928. He is describing rationing in Petrograd in 1918
>
> The rations were minute: black bread, a few herrings each month, a very small quantity of sugar for people in the 'first category' (workers and soldiers) and none at all for the 'third category' (non-workers). Last winter was torture – no heating, no lighting and the ravages of famine.

Bolshevik reforms

The Bolsheviks also faced opposition from different parts of Russian society who opposed their reforms and early decrees (see page 40).

- The decree on land meant that land was seized from nobles, landlords and the Church. Many of these supported the **Whites** during the Civil War.
- The decree on peace alienated nationalists who wanted to continue the war and objected to losing land to the Germans. Many fought against the Bolsheviks in the Civil War.
- The decree on banking meant bankers and industrialists who lost their wealth and businesses supported the opponents of the Bolsheviks.

The Constituent Assembly

In addition, the decision to dissolve the Constituent Assembly in 1918 did not win the Bolsheviks any friends (see page 41). The Social Revolutionaries (SRs) and **Cadets** accused the Bolsheviks of seizing power by force and demanded the re-calling of the Assembly. They were furious with the Bolsheviks and eventually supported the Whites during the Civil War.

The Treaty of Brest-Litovsk

The Treaty greatly increased the opposition to the Bolsheviks. As we have seen (see pages 44–45), it encouraged many Russians to join anti-Bolshevik groups.

Opponents of the Bolsheviks

Growing opposition to the Bolsheviks caused by economic hardship and Lenin's reforms hardened into civil war in the early summer of 1918. There is no specific date that marks the start of the Civil War but, by May 1918, events escalated when the **Czech Legion** revolted. The Czech Legion comprised about 42,000 soldiers who had fought on the Russian side during the First World War. The Allies convinced the Bolsheviks to transport them across Russia in order to re-join the Allies on the **Western Front**. The presence of this foreign army making its way across Russia was not welcome to local **soviets** – and there was fierce fighting along the route. This led to the Czech troops rebelling and taking over the Trans-Siberian railway. All this encouraged the Whites to come out openly against the Bolshevik regime.

The Whites

The Whites is the collective name for those Russian groups who opposed the Bolsheviks (the Reds). They consisted of:

- former tsarists, nationalists, nobles, landowners and wealthy industrialists who wanted the restoration of the tsar
- liberals and moderate **socialists** who wanted the Bolsheviks defeated and law and order re-established
- Social Revolutionaries who wanted the restoration of the Constituent Assembly.

The Whites had some military support from ex-tsarist generals and were in a position to fight the Bolsheviks (see Figure 6.1, page 50). The Czech Legion gave its support to the White generals.

The Greens

Other opponents of the Bolsheviks were the national minorities, such as the Georgians, who saw an opportunity to establish their independence from Russia. If the Bolsheviks were weak and could be attacked on many fronts, then independence was a possibility. Those who fought the Bolsheviks as groups seeking independence from Russia were known as the Greens.

There were a number of different factions involved in the civil war against the Bolsheviks

Foreign powers

The final group of opponents were foreign powers. Russia's ex-allies: Britain, France, the USA and Japan, all intervened in the war to support the Whites for several reasons:

- Lenin had withdrawn from the war and signed the Treaty of Brest-Litovsk.
- The Bolsheviks cancelled payments of all loans given by the Allies to Russia.
- Britain, France and the USA feared the spread of communism to their own countries.

ОБМАНУТЫМЪ БРАТЬЯМЪ

▲ **Source C** A Bolshevik poster of 1918 showing the Red Army fighting a many-headed monster which represents the different groups that opposed Lenin, including the tsar

ACTIVITIES ?

1 Put together a concept map summarising the main economic and political reasons for the growth of opposition to the Bolsheviks.

2 Which group posed the most serious threat to the Bolsheviks? Draw concentric circles and rank order the different groups who opposed the Bolsheviks, beginning with the most serious in the centre circle. Explain your decisions.

3 What can you learn from Source C about opposition to the Bolsheviks in 1918?

Practice question

How useful are Sources A and B for an enquiry into the situation in Petrograd in 1918? Explain your answer, using Sources A and B and your knowledge of the historical context. (*For guidance, see pages 85–87.*)

6.2 Key events of the Civil War

At first the Civil War did not go well for the Reds. They suffered defeat after defeat in 1918 and early 1919 and were attacked on all sides by White armies led by experienced commanders and supported by foreign powers:

- General Yudenich, with British support, attacked from the north-west and threatened Petrograd.
- General Deniken, supported mainly by the French, threatened the south.
- With British support, Admiral Kolchak attacked from the east.

However, in 1919 the tide began to turn as Figure 6.1 shows.

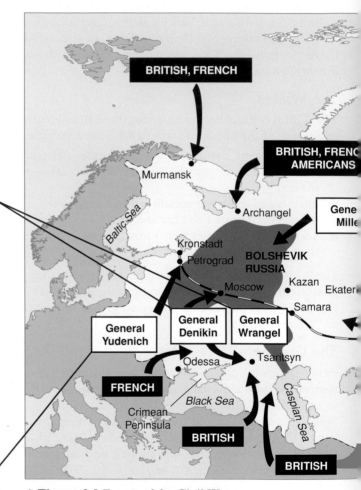

▲ **Figure 6.1** Events of the Civil War

White Generals Denikin and Wrangel in the south

Denikin had an army of 150,000 men, which included a great number of Cossacks from the Don region. His army advanced through the Don region and aimed to link up with Kolchak's army in the east. By the summer of 1918, Denikin's army was besieging Tsaritsyn. This city was vital to the Reds in order to protect grain supplies and prevent the link between the southern and eastern White armies. It was successfully defended by the Bolsheviks under the leadership of Stalin. Denikin launched another offensive in 1919, which got to within 320 km of Moscow. It was defeated by a Red counter-attack led by Trotsky and driven back to the Crimean Peninsula. Denikin was replaced by Wrangel who held out until the following November 1920 when he was evacuated by British and French ships.

White General Yudenich in the West

General Yudenich's army was the smallest army, only some 15,000 men. It reached the outskirts of Petrograd in October 1919 with the support of Estonian troops who wanted independence from Russia. However, Yudenich failed to secure the Petrograd Railway, which allowed the Bolsheviks to send in massive reinforcements to prevent the fall of the city. The Bolsheviks also secured a separate **armistice** with the Estonian forces by promising to recognise Estonian independence. Without the support of Estonia, Yudenich dissolved his armies in mid-1920.

White Admiral Kolchak in the east

Admiral Kolchak led an army of about 140,000 men which advanced from the east, supported by the Czech Legion. At first he was very successful and, by June 1919, had captured Kazan and Samara. However, by the autumn of 1919 the Red Army had forced Kolchak to retreat and in the following year he was captured and shot. This defeat was due to the determined counter-attacks by the Red Army as well as differences and quarrels with the Czechs.

White General Miller in the north

After the Bolshevik takeover, Miller, a general in the Tsarist army, fled to Archangel and declared himself Governor-General of Northern Russia. In May 1919, Admiral Kolchak appointed him to be in charge of the White army in the region where his anti-Bolshevik army was supported by British forces. However, after an unsuccessful advance against the Red Army along the Northern Dvina River in the summer of 1919, British forces withdrew from the region and Miller's men faced the enemy alone, eventually being evacuated to Norway in February 1920.

ACTIVITIES ?

1. Using the map (Figure 6.1), make a timeline of the events of the Civil War.
2. List the strengths and weaknesses of the Reds and the Whites.

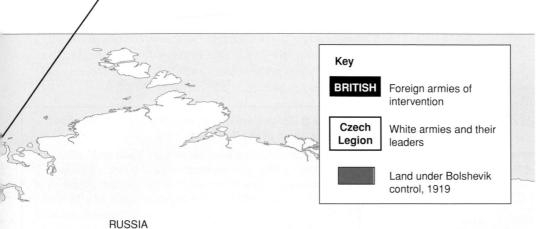

Key

BRITISH	Foreign armies of intervention
Czech Legion	White armies and their leaders
▓	Land under Bolshevik control, 1919

RUSSIA

General Semenov

Trans-Siberian Railway

iral hak

Omsk

Czech Legion

AMERICANS, JAPANESE

Vladivostok

N

CHINA

0   1000 km

White General Semenov in the east

Semenov commanded White forces in the Siberian region supported by Japanese forces. After the defeat of the White movement, Admiral Kolchak transferred power to Semenov in the Far East. However, Semenov was unable to keep his forces in Siberia under control: they stole, burned, murdered and raped civilians, and developed a reputation for being little better than thugs. In July 1920 the Japanese Expeditionary Corps started their withdrawal, leaving Semenov without support. He was defeated by units of the Red Army in October 1920.

EFFECTS OF THE CIVIL WAR

The Civil War had left Russia, especially the economy, in ruins. The transport system was near to collapse which meant that factories could not get the materials they needed and had to close down. Grain production had fallen to very low levels. There was not enough food for the towns and some peasants began to hide any surpluses for their own benefit. There was widespread famine with more people dying of hunger during the Civil War than the fighting. Furthermore, hundreds of thousands died from diseases such as typhus, cholera and dysentery. There was growing and increasingly widespread opposition to **War Communism** (see pages 61–62).

6.3 Reasons for the Bolshevik victory

The Bolshevik victory in the Civil War was due to their own strengths as well as the weaknesses of the opposition, the Whites.

Strengths of the Bolsheviks

The main strengths of the Reds were the leadership of Lenin and Trotsky, their control of the railways, widespread support from the peasants through propaganda and their more negative policies of War Communism (see pages 61–62) and terror.

The leadership of Lenin

The Bolsheviks benefited from the centralised and unified leadership of Lenin and Trotsky. Lenin was the inspirational figure who provided the central political leadership and direction. He was also extremely ruthless in conducting the war, as shown by the introduction of War Communism and the use of the *Cheka* (secret police).

War Communism and the *Cheka*

War Communism meant that ruthless discipline was enforced in factories and strict food rationing was introduced, with the largest rations going to the **Red Army**. All necessary resources were poured into the army – even if this meant peasants and workers went hungry. The *Cheka* terrified ordinary Russians – those found to have helped the Whites could expect no mercy.

The role of Trotsky

In contrast to the various armies and commanders that opposed the Bolsheviks, the Reds had one commander, Trotsky, and one army, the Red Army. Trotsky, appointed **Commissar** of War in March 1918, was key to the success of the Reds. He was able to inspire and rally men and restore discipline and professionalism into what he now called the 'Workers' and Peasants' Red Army' and turn it into an effective fighting force. Trotsky:

- restored **conscription** for men aged 18–40 in order to raise a large army. The Red Army eventually had some 5 million troops
- reintroduced a traditional officer structure and brought back thousands of former tsarist officers, now unemployed and poor and wanting to get back into a job they knew. To ensure their loyalty, Trotsky had their families kept hostage
- promoted talented soldiers who had never made officers in the nobility-dominated tsarist army. These men became the Red Army's best generals
- appointed a Bolshevik political commissar to each army unit to ensure the officers were following the **party line**
- restored strict military discipline, bringing back the death penalty for a range of offences.

Trotsky was not a backroom commander who remained far behind enemy lines. Travelling in a specially equipped train, he rushed to points where the fighting was at its fiercest to provide support. His presence seemed to make a difference, serving to inspire the troops.

As well as setting up and organising the Red Army, Trotsky also decided the overall strategy of the Bolsheviks. This was to defend the Red Army's internal lines of communication and to deny the Whites the opportunity to concentrate large forces in one location. Bolshevik control of the railways was the key to this strategy. Most of the decisive battles between the Whites and Reds took place near rail heads and depots.

> **Source D** Trotsky, writing in his memoirs in 1930, about the setting up of the Red Army
>
> We were constructing an army all over again and under fire at that ... What was needed for this? It needed good commanders – a few dozen experienced fighters, a dozen or so communists ready to make any sacrifice; boots for bare-footed, a bath house, propaganda, food, underwear, tobacco and matches.

▲ **Source E** Trotsky (left) on his special train, visiting Red Army troops during the Civil War

Practice question

Give two things you can infer from Source D about Trotsky's role in the Civil War. (*For guidance, see page 77.*)

Control of the central area and railways

As you can see from Figure 6.1 on pages 50–51, the Reds occupied the central Russian-speaking area of the country. This made territory easier to control and ensured that they had to travel shorter distances.

- They moved their capital to Moscow, at the hub of the railway network. The Reds made better use of the railway network than the Whites to transport men and munitions to the battlefronts.
- Most of the population lived in the central areas, making it easier to conscript more people into the army as they were needed. Red armies often vastly outnumbered their White opponents.
- The central area also contained the main armaments factories in Russia, so the Bolsheviks could carry on producing war materials. Trains could move raw materials and finished goods more easily than road transport. The stores of the tsarist army and the tsar's old **arsenals**, which contained 2.2 million rifles, 12,000 field guns and a great deal of ammunition, fell into their hands.

Support from the peasantry

The support of the peasants was crucial, since they supplied the main body of soldiers on both sides. They had little love for either side, but were often more inclined to support the Bolsheviks for the reasons below:

- Lenin had introduced the Decree on Land in 1917 (see page 40), which gave the peasants the right to the land, whereas the Whites made it clear that they would restore the land to its former owners. The White Admiral Kolchak even gave estates to landlords who had not owned them before the **revolution**.
- The brutality of the White armies drove many peasants to support the Bolsheviks as the lesser of two evils. For example, the **Cossacks** in the southern White army practised 'ethnic cleansing', driving out thousands of non-Cossack peasants, especially Russians and Ukrainians, from their lands and treating them brutally.

Propaganda and a cause

One of the most important factors explaining the success of the Reds, was their driving sense of purpose. They were fighting for a cause – the preservation of the October Revolution – and this, alongside the leadership of Lenin and Trotsky, often resulted in much higher morale and dedication in the Red Army compared to that of their opponents.

In addition, the Bolsheviks made very effective use of propaganda, using imaginative and powerful images, such as those in Source F, and statements such as:

- the Whites would take away land from the peasants
- foreign invaders were supporting the Whites and would control Russia (see propaganda poster Source C on page 49)
- the Reds offered a wonderful new society for workers and peasants.

> **ACTIVITIES** ?
>
> 1 How important were the different strengths of the Bolsheviks in helping them to win the Civil War? Make a list of the main reasons from these two pages (use the sub headings to help you) and give each a rating of 1–5, with 5 being the highest. Briefly explain the decision for your rating.
>
> 2 Study Source F.
>   a) What is the message of the cartoon?
>   b) Devise a caption that the Bolsheviks could have used for this cartoon.

▲ **Source F** Bolshevik poster showing the Whites as dogs, on leads held by the Allied Powers (the USA, France and Britain). The dogs are named Denikin, Kolchak and Yudenich

Weaknesses of the Whites

The success of the Bolsheviks in the Civil War was greatly assisted by the weaknesses of their opponents.

Lack of unity

The Whites were made up of many different political parties who constantly squabbled and did not trust each other. They were never more than an un-co-ordinated collection of separate forces whose morale was never high.

- They could not agree on whether they were fighting for tsarism or republicanism or for the Constituent Assembly. This made it hard for them to co-operate and impossible to develop a common political aim.
- They had little chance of developing a co-ordinated military strategy. Often the White generals would not work together because they did not like or trust each other. This played right into the hands of Trotsky, who was able to deal with each White army in turn, rather than a joint, simultaneous attack on all fronts.
- They lost the support of nationalist groups. White leaders wanted to restore the Russian empire with its pre-1917 borders. This antagonised separatist groups such as the Ukrainians and Georgians who were looking for greater self-government, if not independence.

Poor leadership

The Whites, for the most part, had poor leaders. No White leader of the stature of Trotsky or Lenin emerged.

- Several were cruel and treated their men with contempt, much the same as the treatment of soldiers during the tsarist regime. Therefore, there was little loyalty from the soldiers, many of whom deserted.
- There were very high levels of corruption and indiscipline in the White armies. For example, in Omsk, where Kolchak was based, uniforms and munitions, supplied by foreign allies, were sold on the black market. Officers lived in brothels and were often under the influence of cocaine and/or vodka.

Geographical spread

The Whites were scattered round the edges of the central area (see Figure 6.2), separated by large distances.

- This made communications difficult, especially moving men and weapons.
- It made it very difficult to co-ordinate the attacks of the various White armies.
- The central area, controlled by the Bolsheviks, was heavily populated. Many of the areas under White control were thinly populated which made it difficult to conscript large armies.
- The Whites did not control the railways and often had to transport troops and supplies across huge distances using very poor roads. They had no telephone links and had to use officers on horseback to convey messages.

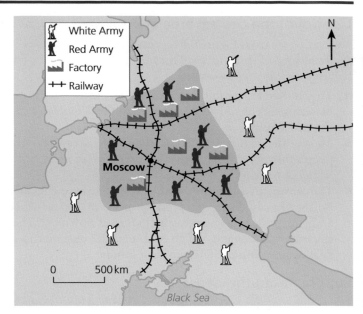

▲ **Figure 6.2** Geographical spread of the Red and White armies

Foreign intervention

Foreign support was half-hearted and ineffective.

- There was lukewarm support from most of the British government and the British public.
- French soldiers were not keen to fight and there were mutinies in the French fleet in the Black Sea.
- The Japanese were more interested in trying to grab some valuable territory than fighting the Bolsheviks.
- Moreover, foreign intervention gave the Bolsheviks a major propaganda opportunity. They could present themselves as the defenders of Russian soil against foreign forces.

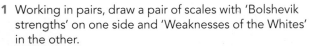

ACTIVITIES

1 Working in pairs, draw a pair of scales with 'Bolshevik strengths' on one side and 'Weaknesses of the Whites' in the other.
   a) One of you complete the section on the strengths of the Bolsheviks.
   b) The other on the weaknesses of the Whites.

2 Which do you think was more important in the Bolshevik victory? Explain your answer.

Practice question

Explain why the Bolsheviks won the Civil War of 1918–21.

You may use the following in your answer:
- The leadership of Trotsky
- The lack of unity in the Whites

You must also use information of your own.

(For guidance, see page 95–96.)

6.4 How far do you agree with one of the interpretations?

This section provides guidance on how to answer the question 'How far do you agree with one of the interpretations?' Look at the question below. Then read the guidance on how to answer it on page 56.

Question

How far do you agree with Interpretation 1 about the events of the Bolshevik Revolution? Explain your answer, using both interpretations and your knowledge of the historical context.

> **Interpretation 1** From *History of the USSR,* by Y. Kukushkin, a Soviet historian, published in 1981. He is describing the attack on the Winter Palace
>
> The signal for the start of the assault was given from the cruiser 'Aurora' which fired a blank shot from her gun. The Red Guards, sailors and soldiers poured from the adjacent streets in an irresistible rush across the square in front of the Winter Palace. The last remnants of the forces that opposed the revolution fell on the night of 25–26 October, 1917. This marked a victory of the armed uprising of the working people in the capital of Russia, Petrograd which began a new era in human history.

> **Interpretation 2** From *A People's Tragedy: The Russian Revolution 1891–1924* by O. Figes, published in 1997
>
> The great October Socialist Revolution was in reality such a small-scale event that it passed unnoticed by the majority of the inhabitants of Petrograd. The legendary storming of the Winter Palace was more like a routine house arrest, since most of the force defending the palace had already left for home, hungry and dejected, before the final attack began. Trotsky himself claimed that 25,000 to 30,000 'at the most' were actively involved – about five per cent of the workers and soldiers in the city.

How to answer

You need to give a balanced answer which agrees and disagrees with the interpretation, using evidence from the two interpretations as well as your own knowledge. Steps on how to answer this question are given below.

Step 1
State the view given in Interpretation 1 using evidence from the interpretation itself.

Example
Interpretation 1 gives the view that the Bolshevik Revolution had mass support and was a popular uprising, through its description of soldiers, sailors and Red Guards pouring through the streets to attack the Winter Palace and calling it an 'armed uprising of working people'.

Step 2
Agree with the view given in Interpretation 1 using your own knowledge. In answer to this question you would need to expand on the example answer with at least one more example of evidence from your own knowledge.

Example
It was certainly the case that the Bolsheviks had support by October 1917 as a result of the activities of Lenin, more especially the April Theses, and Trotsky. Their promise of peace, land and reform appealed to many Russians, especially the working classes in the towns and cities. Indeed, membership of the Bolshevik Party had increased from 24,000 in February 1917 to 340,000 by October of that year.

Step 3
Disagree with the view given in Interpretation 1 using evidence from Interpretation 2. In answer to this question you would need to expand on the example answer with at least one more example of evidence from Interpretation 2.

Example
Interpretation 2 challenges the view that the Bolshevik takeover was a popular uprising shown by the mass attack on the Winter Palace. Rather, it suggests that it was an uprising which few noticed or were involved in, with Trotsky himself suggesting that as few as 30,000 took part. The capture of the Winter Palace was not achieved by a mass attack but by a routine house arrest.

Step 4
Disagree with the view given in Interpretation 2 using your own knowledge. See if you can add to the example given with more evidence from your own knowledge.

Example
There was not mass support for the Bolshevik Revolution as the Bolsheviks had limited support in Petrograd and the rest of Russia. This limited support is shown in the November elections for the Constituent Assembly that followed, where the Bolsheviks obtained less than a quarter of the seats. Even though membership of the party had grown since the return of Lenin, it was still only 340,000 out of a total Russian population of about 125 million. There was no mass storming of the Winter Palace. Bolshevik soldiers filtered into the palace by various entrances and wandered the corridors disarming the few remaining cadets, who put up little resistance.

Step 5
You now need to make a final judgement on the view given in Interpretation 1.

Example
Overall, I agree (or disagree) with the view given in Interpretation 1 because ...

6.5 Further examination practice on interpretations

Here is an opportunity to practise answering some more interpretation questions.

▲ **Source A** A Bolshevik poster of 1919 which is praising the 3-million strong Red Army

Source B From a report by Robert Bruce Lockhart, a British agent in Russia during the Civil War, November 1918

It must be admitted that the success of Bolshevism in Russia is due to more deep-rooted causes than the terrorism of a band of workers. The Bolshevik supporters may not number more than 10 per cent of the population but their worst enemies cannot deny their energy and their party discipline.

Interpretation 1 From *History of the USSR*, Y. Kukushkin, a Soviet historian, published in 1981

The Communist Party sent its best members to join the Red Army. By the end of 1918 the Red Army was over 1,700,000 strong. It was a formidable force. Even so, on every battlefront Red Army units had to fight against an enemy who was better equipped, better trained and numerically superior.

Interpretation 2 From *Communist Russia under Lenin and Stalin*, C. Corin and T. Fiehn, published in 2002

The Bolsheviks had a single, unified command and Trotsky organised the Red Army into an effective fighting force. They held control of the central area which included Petrograd and Moscow and moved their capital to Moscow, at the hub of the railway system. This made it easier to transport men and munitions to the battle front.

Question 1

Study Interpretations 1 and 2. They give different views about the reasons for the Bolshevik victory in the Civil War. What is the main difference between these views? Explain your answer, using details from both interpretations.

> ■ You need to give the views of each interpretation and back these up with evidence from each one.

Question 2

Suggest **one** reason why Interpretations 1 and 2 give different views about the reasons for the Bolshevik victory in the Civil War. You may use Sources A and B to help explain your answer.

> The interpretations may differ because:
> ■ they have given weight to two different sources. You can use evidence from Sources A and B for this answer. Match the sources to the interpretations
> ■ they are partial extracts and in this case they do not actually contradict one another
> ■ the authors have a different emphasis.

Question 3

How far do you agree with Interpretation 2 about the reasons for the Bolshevik victory in the Civil War? Explain your answer, using both interpretations and your knowledge of the historical context.

> You need to give a balanced answer which agrees and disagrees with the interpretation using evidence from the two interpretations as well as your own knowledge.
> ■ State the view given in Interpretation 2 using evidence from the Interpretation itself.
> ■ Agree with the view given in Interpretation 2 using your own knowledge.
> ■ Disagree with the view given in Interpretation 1 using evidence from the Interpretation.
> ■ Disagree with the view given in Interpretation 1 using your own knowledge.
> ■ Make a final judgement on the view given in Interpretation 2.

By 1924, the USSR was governed by a centralised, one-party dictatorship which did not permit anyone to challenge its power. Within months of seizing power, Lenin introduced War Communism as a method of controlling the economy as well as supplying the needs of the Red Army during the Civil War. This proved extremely unpopular with the peasants and led to opposition to the Bolsheviks, who replaced War Communism with The New Economic Policy (NEP). There were also significant social changes during the years 1918–24.

7.1 Moves towards totalitarianism

In the years 1918–24, Lenin was able to establish a dictatorship, partly through the use of the Red Terror and the *Cheka* but also through centralised control of all aspects of Russian society.

The Red Terror and the role of the *Cheka*

The systematic use of terror was used by Lenin (see Source A) to back up any new measures, remove any opposition to the Bolshevik regime and establish a one-party state (see page 59).

In December 1917, Lenin used *Sovnarkom* to set up the 'All-Russian Extraordinary Commission for Combating Counter-revolution and Sabotage.' This became known as the *Cheka*, its head was Felix Dzerzhinsky and it was responsible for dealing with law and order and political opposition to the Bolsheviks. It was the Bolshevik secret police, answerable directly to Lenin who gave it unlimited powers. Initially it had 100 operatives, but by 1921 it had 30,000.

Lenin and Dzerzhinsky (see Source B) used the *Cheka* to remove opponents of the Bolshevik regime and to shoot army deserters. Members of the other main political parties were arrested and removed from political activities. Following an attempt on Lenin's life at the end of August 1918, Dzerzhinsky began what is known as the Red Terror, in which those suspected of working against the revolution were arrested, tortured and executed.

- Its victims included large numbers of workers and peasants as well as princes, priests, judges, merchants, traders and even children.
- In Petrograd alone over 800 so-called enemies of the state were executed.
- In the cities, *Cheka* arrests were often terrifyingly random in nature, for example simply being an acquaintance of a suspect.
- The *Cheka* was even more active in the countryside, supporting requisition brigades (see page 61).
- Opponents were imprisoned in concentration and labour camps.

By the end of 1918, the *Cheka* had 'removed' more than 50,000 people. There were numerous stories about its cruelty, including one example in Kharkov where members of the *Cheka* scalped their prisoners, and another, in Poltava, where they burnt at the stake peasants who opposed them. It thus created a climate of fear and terror not only across Russia but even within the Bolshevik Party, making it difficult to criticise the government. Hence the *Cheka* enabled Lenin to retain power at a most difficult time. By the end of the Civil War, an estimated 200,000 had been killed and a further 85,000 put in prison by the secret police (see Source C).

ACTIVITY ?

What was the role of the *Cheka* under Lenin?

Source A From a letter written by Lenin to a Bolshevik leader in Penza in 1919

Hang no fewer than a hundred well-known *kulaks*, richbags and blood-suckers and make sure the hanging takes place in full view of the people.

Source B From an interview given by Dzerzhinsky, the leader of the *Cheka*, to the press in 1918

The *Cheka* is the defence of the revolution as the Red Army is; as in the civil war, the Red Army cannot stop to ask whether it may harm particular individuals, but must take into account only one thing, the victory of the revolution over the bourgeoisie. So the *Cheka* must defend the revolution and conquer the enemy even if its sword falls occasionally on the innocent.

Source C From *Memoirs of a British Agent* by Bruce Lockhart published in 1932. Lockhart was in Moscow in 1918 and describes what he saw when being questioned by the *Cheka* in August 1918

As we were talking a motor van pulled up in the courtyard below. There was a scream. Then the fat figure of a priest was half pushed and half carried to the van. His terror was pitiful. Tears rolled down his face. His knees rocked and he fell, like a great ball of fat, on the ground. I felt sick and turned away. It was the notorious Bishop Vostorgoff, one of the several hundred victims of the Red Terror who were shot at the time as revenge for the attempted assassination of Lenin.

▲ **Source D** Members of *Cheka*, 1919. Fourth from left is Felix Dzerzhinsky

Bolshevik centralisation

With the help of the Red Terror, Lenin was able to create a dictatorship of the Communist Party in the years after the October Revolution. However, this was also achieved through political **centralisation** – central control through the **Politburo** – and economic centralisation, which we examine in the next section (pages 61–63).

The role of the Politburo

The Communist Party controlled the government at every level. Key officials in the government were members of the Communist Party and senior members of the government were usually senior members of the Party.

The Politburo was the leading decision-making body of the Communist Party. It was set up in 1919 and made all the key decisions, exercising complete control over the government. It met on a daily basis and initially consisted of five members chosen by the **Central Committee** of the Bolshevik Party. It was intended to make day-to-day decisions which were too urgent to wait for Central Committee debate. However, all major decisions, under Lenin's leadership, were increasingly made by the Politburo.

Lenin's role

Lenin realised the need for strong government, especially because of the threats posed by the opposition to Bolshevik rule immediately after the October Revolution, as well as during the subsequent Civil War. He was the driving force behind the early Bolshevik decrees and the increasing Bolshevik centralisation in the desperate struggle for survival. Lenin was not a believer in democracy and was convinced that the Bolshevik Party had both the duty to direct the people and the right to obedience from them. During the Civil War, when there was a desperate need for quick decisions, central power and decision-making became increasingly concentrated on Lenin himself and the Politburo.

Practice questions

1 Give two things you can infer from Source A about the *Cheka* and the Red Terror. (*For guidance, see page 77.*)
2 How useful are Sources B and C as evidence of the *Cheka*? Explain your answer, using Sources B and C and your knowledge of the historical context. (*For guidance, see pages 85–87.*)

Lenin's death

On 25 May 1922, Lenin had a stroke which left him partially paralysed on his right side and temporarily unable to speak. His illness meant that he could not take an active role in government for some months. Instead, during the summer of 1922, Russia was ruled by a group of three of the leading Bolsheviks, Stalin, Zinoviev and Kamenev.

Lenin resumed limited duties in August and was able to address party meetings. However, he suffered a second stroke on 15 December 1922. A third stroke followed on 9 March 1923 and this resulted in almost complete loss of speech – he could only say words of one syllable – and was confined to a wheelchair. His contribution to Russian politics was over. He died in January 1924.

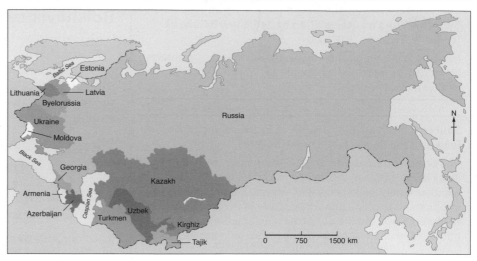

▲ **Figure 7.1** The USSR (Soviet Union) in 1922

Practice question

Explain why Lenin was able to establish a dictatorship of the Communist Party in the years 1918–24.

> You may use the following in your answer
> - The *Cheka*
> - The Politburo
>
> You must also use information of your own.

(For guidance, see pages 95–96.)

THE SETTING UP OF THE USSR

The Union of Soviet Socialist Republics (USSR) or the Soviet Union was officially set up in 1922. This included areas occupied by the **Red Army** during the Civil War as well as areas with a history of independence such as Georgia and the Ukraine (see Figure 7.1).

▼ **Source E** On Stalin's orders, Lenin's body was embalmed in 1924 and placed in a coffin in a Mausoleum in Red Square, the centre of Moscow. It was put on public display there and can still be visited today

7.2 War Communism

War Communism was introduced in 1918 as a method of controlling the economy in order to make sure every area of economic life was focused on supplying the needs of the Red Army and winning the Civil War. War Communism was not one particular law passed by the Bolsehviks; it was a whole series of harsh measures by which the government took control of the economy. It was introduced for several reasons, as outlined in Table 7.1.

▼ **Table 7.1** Reasons why War Communism was introduced

Economic	Social	Political	Military
The peasants wanted to keep the land they had been given but were unwilling to sell the food they grew. Lenin wanted to control the supply of food for the towns. Prices had risen rapidly and there was inflation.	There were severe shortages of food and other basic necessities in Russia.	The policy followed the Communist idea of central control and direction of the economy.	The Bolsheviks had to guarantee supplies for the huge Red Army during the Civil War against the **Whites**.

Features of War Communism

War Communism meant that the government controlled every aspect of economic life. Its main features are described below.

- Rationing of food in cities was to be strictly applied during food shortages.
- Private trading was banned. Peasants could no longer sell their surplus food for profit but had to give it to the government. Lenin ordered requisition squads into the countryside to seize food if peasants proved unwilling to surrender their produce.
- Factories with more than 10 workers were nationalised. This meant that the state now owned the factories and decided how much was to be produced in each industry. Workers were under government control and could be told where to work. Industry was put under the control of *Vesenkha* – the Supreme Economic Council, which reported directly to *Sovnarkom* – the **Council of People's Commissars**. By the autumn of 1919, it was estimated that 80 per cent of enterprises were controlled by the government.
- Rapid inflation led to money becoming valueless. People had to barter, which meant exchanging goods rather than using money.

◄ **Source F** A Bolshevik poster of 1919 to encourage the requisition squads used to seize food in the countryside. The poster reads: 'You shed your blood for the workers' and peasants' revolution. The workers and peasants will deny themselves and give you their last clothes and boots. Take them!'

ACTIVITY ?

Study Source F. What is the message of the poster? Would the peasants have agreed with this message? Explain your answer.

ACTIVITIES ?

1 What does Table 7.2 suggest about the effects of War Communism?

2 Why did War Communism encourage opposition to the Bolsheviks?

Reasons for War Communism's unpopularity

It was vital that the Red Army was supplied with the weapons and food which it needed to fight the war effectively, and War Communism was very effective in keeping the army supplied. So, in theory, Lenin's decision to introduce War Communism was sound, but practically it was flawed. It was unpopular with peasants and workers and led to widespread starvation. Peasants did not respond well to the idea of giving up produce to the state, and so they grew less and bred fewer animals, leading to a fall in agricultural output (see Table 7.2). When Lenin sent armed Bolsheviks into the countryside to carry out **food requisitioning** by force, the peasants resisted fiercely (see Source H). Lenin's answer to this was to turn other peasants against those who refused to hand over their grain. He called these peasants, *kulaks,* which means tight-fisted (see Source I).

The Bolsheviks even took the grain needed for sowing for the next crop. The result was a terrible famine in 1920–21 in which it is estimated 7 million peasants and workers died (see Source J).

These policies encouraged opposition to the Bolsheviks, especially as it was very difficult to tell the difference between a *kulak* and an ordinary peasant. A group called Workers' Opposition was formed to press for changes to the policy. One of the group's calls was for 'Soviets without Communists'. Whereas Lenin's original land decrees (see page 40) had won the Bolsheviks support from the peasants, War Communism lost much of this support.

▼ **Table 7.2** Industrial and agricultural output in Russia, 1913 and 1921

Output in millions of tonnes	1913	1921
Grain	80	37.6
Sugar	1.3	0.05
Coal	29	8.9
Iron	4.2	0.1
Steel	4.3	0.2
Oil	9.2	3.8
Electricity (in million kWh)	2039	520

▲ **Source G** A White Russian poster of 1919, depicting food requisitioning

Source H From *Memoirs of a Revolutionary*, V. Serge, 1945. Here he is writing about food requisitioning

Groups which were sent into the countryside to obtain grain by requisition might be driven away by the peasants with pitchforks. Savage peasants would slit open a Commissar's belly, pack it with grain, and leave him by the roadside as a lesson to all.

Source I From a speech by Lenin to workers in Petrograd in August 1918

These bloodsuckers have grown rich during the war on the people's wants ...These spiders have grown fat at the expense of the peasants ...These leeches have drunk the blood of workers. Growing richer the more the workers starved in the cities and factories ... Merciless war against these *kulaks*. Death to them

Source J From *My Disillusionment in Russia, 1923*. This was written by an American woman, E. Goldman, who returned to Petrograd in 1920. She had lived in Russia in the 1880s but then went back to the USA

It was almost in ruins, as if a hurricane had swept over it. The streets were dirty and deserted. All life had gone from them. The people walked about like living corpses. The shortage of food and fuel was slowly sapping the city. Grim death was clutching at its heart. Emaciated and frostbitten men, women and children were being whipped by a common lash, the search for a piece of bread or a stick of wood. It was a heart-rending sight by day, and oppressing weight by night. It fairly haunted me, this oppressive silence broken only by the occasional shots.

ACTIVITY

Work in pairs. You live in Russia in 1920 and are an opponent of War Communism.
   a) Using evidence from these two pages one of you write a letter to *Pravda*, the official government newspaper, criticising the policy. (*Pravda* meaning 'truth' was the leading newspaper of the Bolshevik government.)
   b) The other write a reply to be published in *Pravda* on behalf of the Bolshevik government.

Practice questions

1   How useful are Sources H and J for an enquiry into the reasons for the unpopularity of War Communism. Explain your answer, using Sources H and J and your knowledge of the historical context. (*For guidance, see pages 85–87.*)
2   Give two things you can infer from Source J about the effects of War Communism. (*For guidance, see page 77.*)

The Kronstadt Mutiny

The greatest challenge for Lenin and Trotsky over War Communism came in March 1921, when there was a rebellion of sailors at the naval base of Kronstadt against the Bolshevik government. Thousands of sailors protested at events in Russia and objected, like the Workers' Opposition, to the way the Communist Party (the Bolsheviks were now called Communists) was taking power away from the **soviets**. Source K shows some of the complaints the sailors had, which led to the following demands:

- Because the present soviets do not express the will of the workers and peasants, new elections should be held.
- Freedom of speech and press to be granted to workers and peasants.
- Freedom of assembly and of trade unions and peasants' associations.
- All political prisoners belonging to **socialist** parties to be set free.

The reaction of the Communist government

Lenin wanted no opposition and decided to stop the protests. The demands of the protestors came as a shock to him, especially as the Kronstadt sailors had proved to be some of his most loyal supporters. Trotsky had to use the Red Army to put down the rebellion. He ordered General Tukhachevsky to attack the naval base using 60,000 troops. During a three-week struggle over 20,000 men were killed or wounded in fierce fighting (see Source L). The surviving rebels were either executed by the *Cheka* or put in a *gulag*. For other opponents, the end of the rebellion meant the end of any hope of removing the Communists.

Lenin realised he had to change the policy – for him, Kronstadt was the 'flash that lit up reality'. In March 1921, Lenin abandoned War Communism and introduced the **New Economic Policy** in its place.

▲ **Source K** A painting showing a meeting of sailors during the Kronstadt Mutiny, March 1921. Extracts from the meeting are shown in the speech bubbles

Source L From a report to Trotsky by the army commander, Tukhachevsky, after the defeat of the sailors

The sailors fought like wild beasts. I cannot understand where they found the might for such rage. An entire company fought for an hour to capture one house and when the house was captured it was found to contain two or three soldiers at a machine gun. They seemed half dead but they snatched their revolvers and gasped, 'We didn't shoot enough of you bastards'.

ACTIVITIES ?

1 Study Source K and the speech bubbles surrounding the painting, giving the grievances of the Kronstadt sailors. Using your knowledge of Lenin's government of 1918–21, explain whether or not you think their grievances were justified.

2 Does Source L suggest that the Kronstadt Mutiny was a serious threat to Communist rule? Explain your answer.

3 Produce a newspaper headline for *Pravda*, the official government newspaper, about the rebellion.

4 Why do you think the rebellion was crushed so quickly and with such brutality?

7.3 The New Economic Policy (NEP)

Lenin introduced the New Economic Policy (NEP) in 1921 to replace War Communism. It was intended primarily to meet Russia's urgent need for food. If the peasants could not be forced to produce food, then they must be persuaded. He also felt that the new policy would give Russia some breathing space after a period of almost eight years' war. There were some communists who felt that they were betraying the revolution by reverting back to capitalism.

The key features of the NEP were:

- peasants would still have to give a fixed amount of grain to the government, but they could sell their surplus for profit again
- peasants who increased their food production would pay less tax
- factories with fewer than 20 workers would be given back to their owners and consumer goods could be produced and sold for profit
- people could use money again and a new rouble was introduced
- key industries, such as coal and steel, still remained under state control
- the electrification of Russia. Lenin was convinced that electrical power was the key to economic growth. A network of power stations was established in the years after 1921.

The NEP also encouraged foreign trade with countries such as Britain. Over the next few years, there were large-scale exchanges of Western industrial goods for Russian oil and wheat.

Reactions to the NEP

At the Tenth Party Congress in 1921, there was a fierce debate about the NEP. Some party members considered it to be a betrayal of the principles of the October Revolution (see Source M). What finally persuaded the doubters was the Kronstadt Munity. They realised that splits in the Party could result in them losing power altogether. There was a genuine desire for unity and they were prepared to support Lenin, as long as the NEP was, as Lenin promised, a 'temporary' measure (see Source N).

> **Source M From *From Lenin to Stalin* written by Victor Serge in 1937. Serge was expelled from the Communist Party in 1928 by Stalin for criticising his policies. Here he was attacking the NEP**
>
> In just a few years, the NEP restored to Russia an aspect of prosperity. But to many of us this prosperity was sometimes distasteful ... we felt ourselves sinking into the mire – paralysed, corrupted ... There was gambling, drunkenness and all the old filth of former times ... Classes were re-born under our eyes ... There was a growing gap between the prosperity of the few and the misery of the many.

> **Source N From a speech by Lenin to party members in March 1921**
>
> We are now retreating, going back as it were, but we are doing this so as to retreat first and then run and leap forward more vigorously. We retreated on this one condition alone when we introduced our New Economic Policy ... so as to begin a more determined offensive after the retreat.

Effects of NEP

By 1922, the results of the NEP were better than anyone had expected.

- There was food in the markets in the cities and a growing trade in other goods.
- Shops, cafes and restaurants reopened.
- By 1923, cereal production had increased by 23 per cent compared to 1920 (see Table 7.3).
- There was a rapid growth in industrial activity, especially from small-scale enterprises. From 1920 to 1923, factory output rose by almost 200 per cent (see Table 7.3).
- Private traders known as 'Nepmen' appeared. They bought up produce such as grain, meat, eggs and vegetables to take into the markets of the cities. They travelled round the workshops picking up nails, shoes, clothes and hand tools to sell in the markets. By 1923, Nepmen handled about three-quarters of the retail trade. By 1923, there were 25,000 private traders in Moscow alone.
- Peasants did well out of the NEP. After the famine, there was rapid recovery in the villages. A great deal of trade in produce and handcrafted goods was encouraged between the villages. Peasants were also able to make money on the side in the cities through the Nepmen. They were able to farm their land without much interference from the government.

▼ **Table 7.3** Agricultural and industrial recovery during the New Economic Policy

	1921	1922	1923	1924	1925
Agriculture					
Sown area (millions of hectares)	90.3	77.7	91.7	98.1	104.3
Grain harvest (millions of tonnes)	37.6	50.3	56.6	51.4	72.5
Industry					
Coal (millions of tonnes)	8.9	9.5	13.7	16.1	18.1
Steel (thousands of tonnes)	183	39	709	1140	2135
Finished cloth (millions of metres)	105	349	691	963	1688
Value of factory output (millions of roubles)	2004	2619	4005	4660	7739
Electricity (millions of kWh)	520	775	1146	1562	2925
Rail freight carried (millions of tonnes)	39.4	39.9	58.0	67.5	83.4
Average monthly wage of urban worker (in roubles)	10.2	12.2	15.9	20.8	25.2

Shortcomings of the NEP

Debate about the NEP continued throughout its existence. However, when Lenin died in 1924, the debate was set to become even fiercer within the Communist Party. Trotsky described the New Economic Policy as the 'first sign of the degeneration of Bolshevism'. One rumour had it that the letters NEP stood for 'New Exploitation of the **Proletariat**'.

Those who criticised the NEP said that a new class was created – 'Nepmen'. This term was applied to those who stood to gain from the capitalism permitted under the new policy: the *kulaks*, the retailers and the small manufacturers. It was said that greed and selfishness were returning to Russia. Nepmen and *kulaks* went against the ideals of the October Revolution and were part of this new get-rich-quick, increasingly capitalist society.

The NEP encouraged corruption and vice because of the new-found wealth for some people. Prostitution and crime flourished. The Moscow municipal government got most of its income from taxes on gambling clubs, which was a symbol of this new decadence.

By 1923, so much food was flooding into the cities that the prices started to drop, while the prices of industrial goods rose because they were still in short supply. Trotsky called this the 'scissors crisis'. He likened the economic problem created by the widening gap between industrial and agricultural goods to the open blades of a pair of scissors. It made the peasants reluctant to buy industrial goods. The crisis did not last long as the government took action to bring the price of industrial goods down.

◀ **Source O** Nepmen in Smolensk market, 1921

Source P Written in the 1980s by Leonid Orlov, a Bolshevik supporter who is remembering life in Russia in the early 1920s

There wasn't a scrap of food in the country. We were down to a quarter of a pound (114 g) of bread per person. Then suddenly they announced the NEP. Cafes started opening as well as restaurants. Factories went back into private hands. It was capitalism. In my eyes what was happening was the very thing I'd struggled against.

ACTIVITIES ❓

1 Working in pairs, study Table 7.3 and Sources M to P (pages 65–67). Which evidence suggests the NEP was a success, and which a failure? Give a brief explanation for each decision.

2 Which of the following statements best sums up the NEP? Give reasons for your choice.
   - The NEP was a popular and successful policy.
   - The NEP was an unpopular but successful policy.
   - The NEP was an unpopular and unsuccessful policy.

Practice questions

1 Give two things you can infer from Source P about the NEP? (*For guidance, see page 72.*)

2 How useful are Sources M (page 65) and P for an enquiry into of the effects of the New Economic Policy? Explain your answer, using Sources M and P and your knowledge of the historical context. (*For guidance, see page 85–87.*)

7.4 Social change

In the years 1918–24, Bolshevik policies had an impact on the lives of many. This section looks at the impact of their policies on women, education and culture.

Women

There were a number of changes for women, some of which actually worsened their position, while others improved their position.

Marriage

Lenin was convinced that the traditional married role of women was nothing better than slavery, with wives the property of their husbands. He passed a series of laws which had a great impact on the lives of women:

- New divorce law which made it far easier to get a divorce.
- Guaranteed paid maternity leave two months before and after the birth.
- In 1920 abortion on demand was made legal in all state hospitals. The USSR became the first country to legalise abortion. Before that, many women had died or been seriously injured in back-street operations.
- Church weddings were replaced with civil marriages which reduced the influence of religion.

Lenin felt that the Soviet government had done more than any other country to emancipate women. However:

- in 1919, the USSR had the highest marriage rate and, by the mid-1920s, the highest divorce rate in Europe, 25 times higher than Britain. By 1927, two-thirds of Moscow marriages ended in divorce.
- with easy divorce available, many women were abandoned when they were pregnant. Men initiated 70 per cent of divorces.

Employment

In employment, on the whole the position of women worsened. During the First World War, the number of women working in industry doubled. However, after the Civil War, with five million men discharged from military service, women suffered as men were given preference for jobs. Indeed, with the growth of urban unemployment, women were forced from skilled to unskilled work, mainly in textiles and domestic service, or unemployment. Furthermore, women in employment often worked an eight-hour day outside the home plus an extra five hours in domestic tasks, as men did not help in the home.

Politics

The Communist Party stressed the equality of women and men. In 1919, the Party set up a Woman's Department of the *Sovnarkom* called the **Zhenotdel**. Its leader, Alexandra Kollontai, was the first woman ever to be a member of a European government. In practice, *Zhenotdel* focused on practical help such as social services and education rather than increased political participation. In reality, women made little progress in politics because of male chauvinism. There were even reports of women being attacked or beaten up by their husbands for being involved in party work.

- In 1917, women formed 10 per cent of party membership. By 1928 this had increased only slightly to 12 per cent.
- At the Party Congress of 1918, only five per cent of the voting delegates were women. The numbers actually fell over the next six years.

Source Q A woman delegate speaking at a party congress in 1923. She complained that her husband forbade her to take part in politics

And in those very meetings which he forbids me to attend because he is afraid I will become a real person – what he needs is a cook and mistress wife – in those very meetings where I have to slip in secretly, he makes thunderous speeches about the role of women in the revolution, calls women to a more active role.

Education

In the 1919 Communist Party Programme education was defined as 'an instrument for the Communist transformation of society'. This was achieved through control of education. Each child was to receive nine years of free, **universal education** schooling, and state-controlled youth organisations were set up.

Schooling

Schools were placed under the Commissariat for Enlightenment.

- The curriculum was changed to include compulsory learning about the history of revolution and communism.
- There was more practical education, focusing on technical subjects and industrial training, with visits to factories, state farms and power stations.
- The authority of teachers was reduced and they were designated as 'school workers'. They were forbidden to set homework or discipline pupils. This led to a lack of authority and discipline in the schools.
- The financial pressure under the NEP meant that the idea of universal schooling had to be abandoned. Many children left school and, by 1923, the number of schools and pupils was barely half that of two years earlier.

Youth organisations

Two youth organisations were set up to capture the hearts and minds of the young through the indoctrination of Communist ideas.

- The Pioneers was for children under 15 and was very much like the Boy Scouts with activities, trips and camping.
- The *Komsomol* was for young people from the age of 15 until their early twenties. This was much more serious and was used by the Communists to take propaganda into the towns and villages through *Komsomol* activities. *Komsomol* membership was seen as a preparation for entry into the Communist Party.

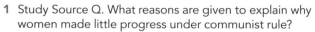

ACTIVITIES

1. Study Source Q. What reasons are given to explain why women made little progress under communist rule?

2. a) Working in pairs, make a copy of and complete the following table about changes in the position of women under the Communists.

	Better	Worse
Marriage		
Employment		
Politics		

   b) Overall, did the position of women improve under the Bolsheviks?

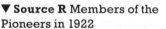

▼ **Source R** Members of the Pioneers in 1922

Culture

The Bolsheviks wanted to control all aspects of culture, but had limited success in the years 1917–24. Following the October Revolution, they set up the Commissariat of Public Enlightenment headed by Anatoly Lunacharsky. He was determined to move away from the 'high art' of the privileged classes – ballet, opera, fine art – to cultural activities which would appeal to a mass audience. He wanted a collective culture, which encouraged workers to produce their own culture.

This new collective culture was known as *Proletkult* (proletariat cultural movement) and was the idea of Lunacharsky's brother-in-law, Alexander Bogdanov. Some of the more extreme members of *Proletkult* wanted to do away with libraries and art galleries, which were seen as symbols of the bourgeois culture of the past. Bogdanov set up studios, poetry circles, folk theatres and exhibitions to encourage the masses to participate in all aspects of culture.

Art

In art, Lenin encouraged artists to depict the life of the Red Army, the workers, the peasants and the heroes of labour. This became known as heroic realism and was later renamed 'Socialist Realism'. It was very optimistic and showed happy workers, working for the victory of communism. The bad side of life was never shown. It was the duty of art to make sure that the message of the revolution was understood by everyone.

Writers

Lenin's government wanted to control writers in Russia and ensure that what was written praised communism. They were not very effective in the 1920s. Writers were allowed to write more or less what they wanted, unless it was regarded as **counter-revolutionary**. The well-known writers continued for a number of years to write as they had done before the revolution.

The cinema

The Bolsheviks made use of the cinema to put across their ideas to the masses. However, cinemas were almost entirely restricted to the towns, so the government introduced specially equipped trains which travelled round Russia showing political propaganda films. In the early 1920s, a special unit, *Proletkino*, was set up to make political films.

Street processions and theatre

The Bolsheviks made use of the rich tradition of street festivals. May Day and the anniversary of the October Revolution became the great annual festivals. Street theatre was used to promote the Party; the most famous example was the re-enactment of the storming of the Winter Palace involving 10,000 people and the Winter Palace itself in October 1920.

◄ **Source S** 'The Bolshevik' painted in 1920 by Boris Kustodiev, an example of a socialist realism painting

Practice question

Explain why there were changes in society in Russia in the years 1918–24.

You may use the following in your answer:
- Women
- Education

You must also use information of your own.

(For guidance, see pages 95–96.)

Stalin's rise to power and dictatorship, 1924–41

KEY
TOPIC 3

This key topic examines the period from the death of Lenin to the involvement of the Soviet Union in the Second World War. It analyses how Stalin became sole leader and removed actual and potential threats to his position, even from within the Bolshevik Party. It analyses how Stalin put in place methods of propaganda and censorship to encourage all Soviet citizens to support his views and ideas.

Each chapter within this key topic explains a key issue and examines important lines of enquiry as outlined in the boxes below.

There will also be guidance on how to answer the inference question (page 77) and the utility question (pages 85–87).

CHAPTER 8 THE STRUGGLE FOR POWER, 1924–28

- The strengths and weaknesses of Stalin and his rivals.
- The emergence of Stalin as leader of the USSR.

CHAPTER 9 THE USE OF TERROR IN THE 1930S

- The reasons for, nature and consequences of the purges, including the purges of the armed forces.
- The work of the secret police (NKVD) and the labour camps.
- The reasons for and importance of the Show Trials, 1936–38.

CHAPTER 10 PROPAGANDA, CENSORSHIP AND THE CULT OF STALIN

- The cult of Stalin – what it was and how it was achieved.
- Propaganda and censorship, including official culture, socialist realism, education and religion and media censorship.
- The new Constitution of 1936.

TIMELINE

1923	*Cheka* renamed OGPU	1929	Rykov, Tomsky and Bukharin removed from the Politburo. Trotsky exiled from the Soviet Union
1924 January	Lenin dies		
1924	Stalin put forward the policy of 'Socialism in One Country'	1934	Murder of Kirov. OGPU renamed NKVD
1925	Trotsky resigned as Commissar for War	1936	New constitution introduced. Beginning of the 'Show Trials'
1927	Zinoviev, Kamenev and Trotsky expelled from the Communist Party	1938	Around 7 million prisoners in labour camps
1928	Purge of Shakhty workers. Stalin undisputed leader of the Soviet Union	1940	Trotsky murdered

Vladimir Lenin died in 1924. There followed a four-year struggle to decide who would succeed him as leader. Trotsky was the favourite due to his leadership of the Red Army and his achievements in the years 1917–24. Stalin was very much the outsider. He was not well known outside political circles, nor did he have Trotsky's intellect and experience. Five others in the Politburo were contenders but, through a combination of his own shrewdness and Trotsky's over-confidence and weaknesses, Stalin had, by 1928, won the leadership contest.

8.1 The strengths and weaknesses of Stalin and his rivals

After Lenin's death in 1924 there was a struggle for power in Russia. There were seven possible candidates to succeed Lenin, of which Stalin was one.

Joseph Stalin

Stalin was born in 1879 in the state of Georgia, the son of a bootmaker. His real name was Joseph Djugashvili. He was from a poor background and had a harsh upbringing. Nevertheless, his mother was determined that he should do well and she worked hard to pay for his education. Indeed, he gained a scholarship to a college for training priests in Tiblisi. However, he lost interest in religion when he discovered **Marxism** and, in 1899, was expelled from the college.

He greatly admired the writings of Lenin and became a member of the **Bolshevik** Party (see page 12), taking the name of Stalin, meaning 'Man of Steel'. In the period after 1902, he became an active revolutionary, taking part in over 1,000 raids to seize money for the party. He was arrested and exiled to Siberia eight times, escaping on seven occasions.

He was freed from exile in 1917 and returned to Petrograd to become editor of *Pravda* (meaning 'Truth'), the Bolshevik newspaper. The evidence suggests he played little role in the **Bolshevik Revolution** of 1917 (see page 30). Nevertheless, he was made **Commissar of Nationalities** in Lenin's government and crushed a rebellion in his own state of Georgia with great brutality. During the Civil War Stalin played an important administrative role in military matters and was instrumental in organising the defeat of the White Army at Tsaritsyn (see pages 52–54).

In 1922, he was given what was regarded as the most boring of jobs, General Secretary of the Bolshevik Party, responsible for the day-to-day running of the Party and the appointment and dismissal of key members.

> **Source A** A Red Army officer writing in 1992 about Trotsky and Stalin after the death of Lenin in 1924
>
> More than anything we were frightened of Trotsky seizing power, though we now know that was not the main problem. In those days Stalin was an unknown figure to us. I worked in the **Kremlin** and I didn't know who Stalin was, and I was a Red Army Commander.

> **Source B** A Communist Party member, Iosti Itskov, talking about Stalin in later years
>
> Stalin tried to stay in the shadows. He was a man whose aim was very clear, but you could not tell how he was going to accomplish it. He accomplished it in the most cunning way. And he allowed nothing to get in his way.

ACTIVITY

Draw up a brief curriculum vitae for Stalin up to 1922. You could use the headings below, or use your own:

- Skills
- Education
- Work experience
- Interests

Practice question

How useful are Sources A and B for an enquiry into Stalin's position in 1924? Explain your answer, using Sources A and B and you knowledge of the historical context. *(For guidance, see pages 85–87.)*

Who were Stalin's leadership rivals?

The seven members of the **Politburo** were all possible candidates for the leadership, but the main five were Trotsky, Bukharin, Kamenev, Zinoviev and Stalin. The two outsiders were Tomsky and Rykov. Trotsky was the favourite and of the main five, Stalin was the long shot.

By 1928, Stalin had emerged as leader. The boxes below show the strengths and weaknesses of Stalin's rivals.

ACTIVITY

Apart from Trotsky, explain which one of the other five rivals was the greatest threat to Stalin. Give reasons for your answer.

Leon Trotsky, 1879–1940

Trotsky had organised the successful Bolshevik Revolution of 1917 (see page 30). He had led the Red Army to success in the Civil War (see page 52). He was extremely intelligent and was eventually chosen by Lenin to be his successor, and was supported by younger Bolsheviks. However, he had been a Menshevik and some Bolsheviks thought him to be arrogant. He also wanted to end the NEP (see page 65).

Lev Kamenev, 1883–1936

Kamenev opposed the Bolshevik Revolution of October 1917, because he felt the time was not right. Nevertheless, he became the leader of the Bolshevik Party in Moscow. He was an ally of Stalin and Zinoviev against Trotsky and was seen as able but lacking in the capacity to lead a country. Like Trotsky, he wanted to end the NEP.

Gregory Zinoviev, 1883–1936

Zinoviev had helped Lenin to set up the Bolshevik Party in 1903. During Lenin's government, he was made the Bolshevik Party chief in Petrograd. He was also Head of the **Comintern**, the organisation through which the Soviet Union tried to bring about Communist **revolutions** in other countries. He was not really liked in the Bolshevik Party and some thought him vain and incompetent. Like Trotsky and Kamenev, he wanted to end the NEP.

Nikolai Bukharin, 1888–1938

Bukharin was a leading Bolshevik who opposed the Treaty of Brest-Litovsk (see page 44). Early in the Revolution, he was on the left of the Party and disagreed with some of Lenin's ideas. He gradually moved towards the Centre and became a firm supporter of Lenin's **New Economic Policy (NEP)**. He wrote several political theory books and was a member of the Politburo after 1924. Lenin liked Bukharin and called him 'the favourite of the whole Party'. He was an open person and lacked political cunning. He wanted to continue the NEP.

Alexei Rykov, 1881–1938

Rykov held many posts after 1917, and was Chairman of the **Council of People's Commissars** (1924–29). He was a very outspoken politician and this lost him support on occasions. He drank a great deal. Like Bukharin, he wanted to continue the NEP.

Mikhail Tomsky, 1880–1936

An early member of the Bolshevik Party, Tomsky was a radical trade unionist. In 1920, he became General Secretary of the **Red International of the Trade Unions**. He became a member of the Politburo in 1922. He had opposed Lenin in major political debates in 1920. Like Bukharin and Rykov, he wanted to continue the NEP. As head of the trade union movement, Tomsky posed a threat to Stalin.

8.2 How did Stalin defeat his rivals?

By early 1923, it was clear that the two main contenders for the leadership were Stalin and Trotsky. Lenins' political **testament** showed he favoured Trotsky (see Source C). Following Lenin's death, his political testament was sent to the Bolshevik **Central Committee**. The diagram on this page shows the steps that led to Stalin defeating his rivals to emerge as leader of the USSR.

> **Source C** Lenin's views on Stalin in his testament, 1923
>
> Comrade Stalin, having become Secretary, has unlimited authority concentrated in his hands and I am not sure whether he will be capable of using that authority with sufficient caution. Comrade Trotsky, on the other hand, is perhaps the most capable man in the present Committee. Stalin is too rude and this fault is not acceptable in the office of Secretary. Therefore I propose to comrades that they find a way of removing Stalin from his post.

Lenin's will and testament

Lenin's testament meant that Stalin had little or no chance of winning the leadership contest. However, he cunningly persuaded other members of the Central Committee, especially Kamenev and Zinoviev, to keep the testament secret for the sake of Party unity and because it also criticised them.

Lenin's funeral

Stalin successfully presented himself as Lenin's close follower. For example, Stalin appeared as the chief mourner at Lenin's funeral, while Trotsky was conspicuous by his absence. Trotsky was ill and Stalin tricked him into believing the funeral was the following day. Trotsky was seen as arrogant and disrespectful of Lenin because he could not be bothered to turn up for his funeral.

Assassination of Trotsky

In 1929 Trotsky was expelled from the Soviet Union. In 1937 he settled in Mexico, where he wrote many articles attacking Stalin, who saw him as a major threat. On 20 August 1940 Trotsky was assassinated by a hired hitman, Ramon Mercador, who put an ice-pick through his head.

'Socialism in One Country'

Stalin worked closely with Zinoviev and Kamenev and, in 1925, they forced Trotsky to resign as Commissar of War. He no longer had control of the Red Army. Moreover, Stalin packed the Congress of Soviets with his supporters to gain support for his policy of 'Socialism in One Country' (see page 75).

Tomsky and Rykov

Tomsky was dismissed from his trade union post in 1929 and eventually committed suicide in 1936, just before being arrested by the secret police. Rykov was gradually removed from his powerful positions and was executed in the purges (see page 78).

Zinoviev and Kamenev

In 1926 Stalin worked with Bukharin and the right wing of the Communist Party, who supported his idea of 'Socialism in One Country', against Zinoviev, Kamenev and Trotsky who, in 1927, were all expelled from the Party.

Bukharin

By 1928 Stalin felt strong enough to turn against Bukharin and his supporters on the right wing of the Party. They supported the NEP, which Stalin wanted to abandon and replace with a new policy of industrial expansion. In 1929, Bukharin was forced to resign. He was executed in 1938 in the purges (see page 78).

Reasons for Stalin's success

Stalin's success was due to a combination of his own strengths and the weaknesses of his rivals, especially Trotsky.

Strengths of Stalin

- Stalin held the key role of General Secretary in the Communist Party. He used this position to appoint officials who supported him and he removed known supporters of Trotsky in order to build up a power base. He soon commanded the support of most Party officials.

- He dominated new members of the Party, especially those he promoted.

- He built up an image of himself as someone who had been close to Lenin, and was therefore his natural successor. He was the chief mourner at Lenin's funeral and made a speech praising him. He had photos published showing him at Lenin's side.

- Stalin cleverly played off his rivals against each other. He knew that Kamenev and Zinoviev feared Trotsky and used their support to remove him. He then allied himself with Bukharin, Tomsky and Rykov and others on the **right wing** of the Party to remove Kamenev and Zinoviev.

- He promoted 'Socialism in One Country', which won popular support within the Communist Party because it suggested that the Soviet Union should concentrate on securing communism at home before it supported revolutions abroad. He attacked Bukharin, Tomsky and Rykov for supporting the NEP and removed them from the Party. This meant, by 1928, he had removed the threats from both the left and right of the Party.

▲ Joseph Stalin

Source D From a conversation between Bukharin and Kamenev at a secret meeting, July 1928

Stalin is an unscrupulous intriguer who sacrifices everything else to the preservation of power ... He changes his theories according to whom he needs to get rid of next.

Source E From *Stalin* by I. Deutscher, published in 1966

In the Politburo, when matters of policy were under debate, Stalin never seemed to impose his views on his colleagues. He carefully followed the course of debate to see what way the wind was blowing and invariably voted with the majority, unless he had assured his majority beforehand.

ACTIVITY

According to Sources D and E, what were Stalin's most important strengths?

Weaknesses of Trotsky

- Trotsky was seen by many Party members as an outsider, partly because he was Jewish, but also because, from 1903 to 1917, he had been a Menshevik, only changing to the Bolshevik Party shortly before the October Revolution.
- Trotsky made a series of tactical mistakes and allowed himself to be out-manoeuvred by Stalin. As leader of the **Red Army**, he was in a powerful position to remove rivals. Instead, he resigned as commander. In addition, he was not prepared to canvas support from his colleagues or rank-and-file members of the Communist Party.
- Trotsky promoted world revolution (**Permanent Revolution**). He wanted the Soviet Union to support communist revolutions in other countries. However, most Russians preferred to concentrate their resources and energy on fully establishing communism in the Soviet Union ('Socialism in One Country').
- He failed to see the leadership question as something which needed a clear focus from him – he seemed to lack urgency or real desire to secure the position of leader.
- He preferred to win arguments and debates by power of intellect and did not like making secret alliances and agreements with colleagues.
- Stalin was underestimated by each of his rivals. He was thought of as a 'grey blur' and someone at the edge and not central to the leadership campaign.

Source F From *Socialism in One Country* by E.H. Carr, published in 1958

Trotsky, the great intellectual, the great administrator, the great orator lacked one quality essential – at any rate in the conditions of the Russian Revolution – to the great political leader. He could encourage and rouse masses of men to acclaim and follow him. But he had no talent for leadership among equals. He could not establish his authority among colleagues by the modest arts of persuasion or by sympathetic attention to the views of men of lesser intellectual calibre than himself.

ACTIVITIES

1 Why might Stalin have encouraged the demonstration shown in Source G?

2 Work in pairs. One of you is Stalin and the other Trotsky. You are to be interviewed by the Politburo members for the job of Party leader. Prepare a presentation/speech for your candidate. Remember to stress your strengths and the weaknesses of your opponent.

3 Re-read pages 72–75.
   a) Create a timeline of how Stalin emerged as leader in the years 1924–28.
   b) Using the information on pages 72–75, annotate your timeline to show where events occurred because of Stalin's strengths or the weaknesses of his rivals, or both.
   c) Give three reasons which you consider to be the most important in Stalin becoming leader of the Soviet Union. Explain your choices.

▲ **Source G** A demonstration against Trotsky

Practice questions

1 Give two things you can infer from Source F about Trotsky's weaknesses as a rival to Stalin in the leadership contest. *(For guidance, see page 77.)*

2 How useful are Sources D (page 75) and F for an enquiry into the emergence of Stalin as leader of the USSR? Explain your answer using Sources D and F and your knowledge of the historical context. *(For guidance, see page 85–87)*

8.3 Inference question

This section provides guidance on how to answer the source inference question.

Question 1

Give two things you can infer from Source A about Stalin.

(4 marks)

> **Source A** From *Assignment in Utopia* by Eugene Lyons, 1937. Lyons was an American journalist.
>
> Whatever I may have thought about the cruelties of his regime, I could not but feel an awed respect for the sharp, single-minded, unfeeling certainty of this man's attitude. Nowhere in it was there so much as a tremor of fellow-feeling for the millions uprooted and dispersed, for the battalions in forced labor camps, for a population stagger under burdens and weakened by deprivations.

How to answer

- You are being asked to give the message or messages of the source, to read between the lines of what is written.
- In addition, you must support the inference. In other words, use details from the source to support the messages you say it gives.
- Begin your answer with 'This source suggests ...' This should help you get messages from the source.
- Aim for two supported inferences to be sure of full marks. For example, in Source A two messages could be:

Question 2

Give two things you can infer from Source B about the death of Lenin.

(4 marks)

> **Source B** From the diary of Walter Duranty, 26 January 1924. Duranty was an American journalist. He is describing people coming to see the dead body of Lenin
>
> What is happening here emphasises the religious aspect of Bolshevism with Lenin as the central figure. How else can one explain the gigantic mass movement to see his body – a movement not of Communists and their sympathisers alone, but of the rest of the population, despite such agony of cold? The Bolsheviks can organise much, but it is not their propaganda which draws these hundreds of thousands to Lenin's feet.

ACTIVITY ❓

Now have a go answering Question 2 using the steps shown for Question 1.

Inference
Source A suggests that Stalin was a determined leader who knew what he wanted.

Support from the source
I know this because the source says that he was single-minded and had a certainty of attitude.

Source A
Whatever I may have thought about the cruelties of his regime, I could not but feel an awed respect for the sharp, single-minded, unfeeling certainty of this man's attitude. Nowhere in it was there so much as a tremor of fellow-feeling for the millions uprooted and dispersed, for the battalions in forced labor camps, for a population stagger under burdens and weakened by deprivations.

Inference 2
Source A suggests that Stalin was not concerned about the human cost of his changes.

Support from the source
I know this because the source says that nowhere was there so much as a tremor of fellow-feeling for the millions uprooted and dispersed.

In the 1930s, Stalin established probably the most effective and ruthless dictatorship of the twentieth century. This involved not only a systematic programme of propaganda, culminating in the 'cult of Stalin', which we will examine in Chapter 10, but also the systematic use of terror to remove any potential threats to his position. Purges of any of Stalin's critics led to the death of millions in the Soviet Union, in which the use of the secret police (NVKD) and labour camps played a key part. Show trials of his main political rivals, where they were forced to confess wrongdoings, were also key feature of the purges in 1936–38.

9.1 The nature of the purges

The purges began in 1932, and became more violent from 1934, leading to the death and imprisonment of millions of Soviet people. No one was immune. Using the secret police, the NKVD (see page 82), Stalin purged anyone who held up, criticised or opposed his plans for collectivisation of agriculture (see page 98) and industrialisation (see page 106). Most of the accused were deported or imprisoned. Some were shot.

The first victims were managers and workers accused of wrecking the first Five-Year Plan for the economy (see page 107), kulaks accused of opposition to collectivisation and ordinary Party members accused of incorrect attitudes. Then, in 1937, the purging of society took on another dimension. People such as artists, musicians, writers, administrators and scientists were accused of acts against the state and arrested. The sentence was either execution or hard labour. As people were arrested and interrogated, their 'confessions' implicated other people and arrests multiplied. Public trials, where the accused were forced to confess their guilt, were a key feature of the purges, particularly from 1936, and served as a warning to other would-be critics.

Figure 9.1 on page 79 shows the key features of Stalin's purges, and Sources A–C give some comment on their nature.

▲ **Source A** A photograph of 1936 from an American newspaper showing the leading Bolsheviks purged by Stalin

Source B A popular joke used during the purges

A man, sitting in his flat, heard a loud knock at the door.

'Who is it?' he asked anxiously.

'It is the Angel of Death.'

'Phew!' the man exclaimed. 'For a moment I thought it was the secret police!'

Source C A French cartoon of the late 1930s, which shows Stalin controlling the purges

ACTIVITIES

1 Look at the flow diagram below. In pairs summarise in one sentence the key feature of each year of the purges identified in the diagram. What does this tell you about the nature of the purges from 1928–38?

2 What can you learn from Source A about Stalin and the purges?

3 Look at Source B. What it the message behind this joke? Can you make up your own joke? (One possibility is a 'knock, knock' type joke.)

4 Study Source C.
   a) What message is the cartoonist trying to get across?
   b) How does the cartoonist achieve this?

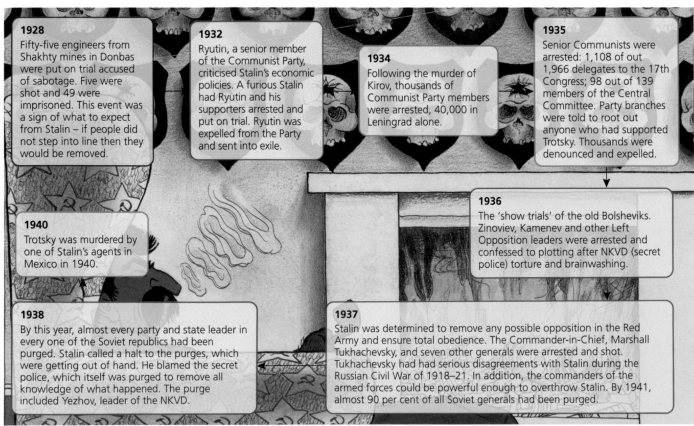

1928
Fifty-five engineers from Shakhty mines in Donbas were put on trial accused of sabotage. Five were shot and 49 were imprisoned. This event was a sign of what to expect from Stalin – if people did not step into line then they would be removed.

1932
Ryutin, a senior member of the Communist Party, criticised Stalin's economic policies. A furious Stalin had Ryutin and his supporters arrested and put on trial. Ryutin was expelled from the Party and sent into exile.

1934
Following the murder of Kirov, thousands of Communist Party members were arrested, 40,000 in Leningrad alone.

1935
Senior Communists were arrested: 1,108 of out 1,966 delegates to the 17th Congress; 98 out of 139 members of the Central Committee. Party branches were told to root out anyone who had supported Trotsky. Thousands were denounced and expelled.

1940
Trotsky was murdered by one of Stalin's agents in Mexico in 1940.

1936
The 'show trials' of the old Bolsheviks. Zinoviev, Kamenev and other Left Opposition leaders were arrested and confessed to plotting after NKVD (secret police) torture and brainwashing.

1938
By this year, almost every party and state leader in every one of the Soviet republics had been purged. Stalin called a halt to the purges, which were getting out of hand. He blamed the secret police, which itself was purged to remove all knowledge of what happened. The purge included Yezhov, leader of the NKVD.

1937
Stalin was determined to remove any possible opposition in the Red Army and ensure total obedience. The Commander-in-Chief, Marshall Tukhachevsky, and seven other generals were arrested and shot. Tukhachevsky had had serious disagreements with Stalin during the Russian Civil War of 1918–21. In addition, the commanders of the armed forces could be powerful enough to overthrow Stalin. By 1941, almost 90 per cent of all Soviet generals had been purged.

▲ Figure 9.1 The key features of the purges. The background image is a 1936 cartoon about the purges

9.2 The reasons for the purges

There was no single reason why Stalin introduced the purges. Indeed, a number of theories and explanations have been given.

1 Threats to his position

Stalin was concerned that his enemies were plotting to overthrow and murder him. His real motive may have been to destroy any men who might form an alternative government – especially the '**old Bolsheviks**' (see Source D).

> **Source D** Bukharin speaking in 1936
>
> Stalin is convinced that he is greater than everyone else. If someone speaks better than he does, that man is for it. Stalin will not let him live, because that man is a constant reminder that he, Stalin, is not the first and best. He is not a man but a devil.

2 Stalin not totally responsible

Others believe that once the purges started they had a snowball effect and were difficult to stop. Stalin may have started them but lost control at local level where they were often used by unscrupulous people to get rid of rivals or those in a coveted superior position.

3 Links with economic policies

Stalin was convinced that he was the only person who could transform the Soviet Union into a modern, industrialised country and that it had to be done quickly. He believed that Hitler would attack the USSR and that it would lose the war if it could not produce enough armaments. Any person who tried to stop him accomplishing this great task was, in Stalin's eyes, a traitor.

One theory argues that the purges and sending people to **labour camps** was the only way Stalin could get mass forced labour for these industrial projects (see page 99). The purges were also a convenient way of excusing setbacks. For example, failures to achieve targets under the Five-Year Plans (see page 107) could be blamed on **sabotage** rather than faults in the Plan.

4 Perceived treachery

It is thought that Stalin purged the armed forces because he suspected the leading officers were spying for Germany and Japan. The leading Soviet general, Tukhachevsky, was executed in June 1937. It is estimated that at least 30,000 members of the armed forces were killed. This included 50 per cent of all army officers.

5 Persecution complex

Some writers, including British writer C. P. Snow, believe Stalin was suffering from a '**persecution** complex' – that he feared everyone was plotting against him. The murder of Kirov is an example of this (see box).

THE MURDER OF KIROV

Stalin decided that his popular **Politburo** colleague, Kirov, was a possible rival. Kirov, a leading communist, spoke at the Seventeenth **Party Congress** in 1934. He criticised Stalin's policy on industrialisation and insisted that it should be slowed down. Kirov's speech was warmly applauded and there was even talk of him replacing Stalin as leader. He was murdered, probably on Stalin's orders. Stalin claimed the murder was part of a plot against him and the Party. The secret police arrested thousands of Kirov's supporters. Kirov's murder marked the start of a new set of more extensive purges against Communist Party members.

◀ **Source E** Soviet leaders carrying the ashes of Kirov. Stalin is front right

Source F Vladimir Alliluyev, Stalin's nephew, was quoted in *Stalin, a Time for Judgement*, by J. Lewis, and insisted his uncle was not involved with the murder of Kirov

Stalin had nothing to do with that murder. My mother was with him when they phoned and informed him that Kirov had been murdered. And my mother said to me, neither before nor after it had she ever seen Stalin in the state he was in after receiving that phone call. And Stalin knew full well that the murder would be linked with his name.

Source G Olga Shatunovskaya, a member of the 1955 commission that inquired into Kirov's death. This was the commission set up by Khrushchev, the Soviet leader, to look into Stalin's crimes

The secret police latched on to the idea that Stalin was dissatisfied after he wrote them a letter saying: 'I am ready for anything now. I hate Kirov.' And they organised the murder. Of course when Stalin found out that some senior Party members had asked Kirov to become leader, he decided to remove him.

ACTIVITIES

1 What does Source D suggest about the reasons for the purges?
2 Study Source E. Suggest reasons why Stalin had this photograph published all over the Soviet Union.
3 Organise the explanations for the purges described on page 80 under the following categories. Do some fall under more than one category? Why might this be the case?

Economic	Political	Psychological

a) Rank order the reasons given for the purges, starting with the most convincing and finishing with the least convincing.
b) Explain your reasons for the first and last in your rank order.

? Practice questions

1 How useful are Sources F and G for an enquiry into the murder of Kirov? Explain your answer, using Sources F and G and your knowledge of the historical context. (*For guidance, see pages 85–87.*)
2 Explain why Stalin carried out the purges in the 1930s.

You may use the following in your answer:
■ Stalin's rivals
■ Forced labour
You must also use information of your own.

(*For guidance, see pages 95–96.*)

9.3 The secret police

As we have seen, in December 1917, the *Cheka* was established and gradually became an instrument of control for the **Bolsheviks**, arresting and killing many thousands of real and alleged opponents of the Bolsheviks in the years 1918–23.

In 1923, the *Cheka* was re-named **OGPU** (and then became the NKVD in 1934). Thus, by the time Stalin was vying for the leadership of the Soviet Union in the 1920s, the secret police had already become an instrument of terror. As leader, Stalin continued to use it as such and made it the cornerstone of his method of control.

Stalin expanded the secret police and gave it greatly increased powers with the 'decree against terrorist acts', issued after Kirov's murder. This meant they could arrest people without charge or trial and execute them on the spot. The secret police were sent out at night and were nicknamed the 'black ravens', because they drove round in black cars. They liked to call in the early hours of the morning.

They were assisted by an army of informers. Even children were encouraged to inform on their parents, neighbours and school friends. Informing on others was a way of showing your loyalty, of settling old scores and of getting someone else's more senior job or position.

The NKVD was used by Stalin to hunt down and destroy his opponents and terrorise ordinary people into obedience. People who were found guilty of opposition or disobedience were sentenced to death, exile or hard labour. It has been estimated that more than a million people were arrested during 1937–38 and about one half of them were shot.

Yezhov, the notorious head of the secret police, and who gave his name to the purging in 1936–38 (*Yezhovschina*) was himself purged in 1938. Yezhov was replaced by his assistant, Lavrenti Beria. He immediately purged the NKVD and appointed friends and ex-colleagues in their places. Stalin appointed Beria Deputy Prime Minister in 1941.

Labour camps

Victims of the purges were sent to labour camps, called *gulags*, which were set up across the Soviet Union, with some in the Arctic Circle. They were run by the secret police. Millions of people were imprisoned and forced to do hard manual work on construction and mining projects.

▲ **Source H** *Gulag* prisoners working in a *gulag* in the mid-1930s. They could work up to 14 hours per day doing exhausting physical work

Source I From the *Gulag Archipelago*, written in 1973 by Alexander Solzhenitsyn. He served time in a labour camp for eight years in the 1940s

In 1938 Ivanor Razannik found 140 prisoners in a cell intended for 25 – with toilets so overburdened that prisoners were taken to the toilet only once a day, sometimes at night. He calculated that for weeks at a time there were three persons per square yard of floor space. In this 'kennel' there was neither ventilation nor a window and the prisoners' body heat and breathing raised the temperature to 40 degrees centigrade. Their naked bodies were pressed against one another and they got eczema from one another's sweat. They sat like that for weeks ... and were given neither fresh air nor water – except for gruel and tea in the morning.

ACTIVITIES

1 Why was the secret police crucial for Stalin in the 1930s?
2 Why did Stalin use *gulags* instead of ordinary prisons?
3 Solzhenitsyn was writing about the *gulags* in a novel. Is Source I still useful as evidence of life in the *gulags* even though it is fiction? Explain your answer.

About 13 million died from cold, hunger and ill-treatment. Living conditions were appalling and food supplies totally inadequate. In 1928, there were around 30,000 prisoners in the labour camps. By 1938, it was around 7 million.

9.4 Show trials

The **show trials** began in 1936. In that year, Stalin began purging the Communist Party of anyone who might oppose him, especially 'old Bolsheviks', such as Kamenev and Zinoviev. Along with 14 others, they were accused of organising Kirov's murder and plotting to assassinate Stalin.

The accused were put on trial in full view of the world. They were forced to confess to a whole range of improbable crimes, including a plot to murder Lenin. The confessions were important because they appeared to show that Stalin was right to purge the Communist Party. Trotsky, now in exile, was accused of leading the plotters.

The show trials helped to create an atmosphere of fear and a sense that not only were enemies of the state everywhere, the police were everywhere too, spying on individuals.

The last of the major show trials was in March 1938 when Bukharin and Rykov were accused. After being found guilty, they were shot.

Confessions

Confessions such as those in Source J did not help the accused, as they were executed after the trials. They confessed because they were physically and psychologically tortured by the secret police (see Source M), and because their families were threatened with imprisonment or death. The prosecutors preferred to have confessions from the accused because they seemed convincing and showed that the state was correct to fear attacks from within.

▲ **Source L** cartoon of the mid-1930s from an American newspaper showing leading Bolsheviks at the show trials

> **Source M** From Eugenia Ginsburg, who was tortured and wrote an account of her treatment in *Journey Into the Whirlwind* in 1968. She was a writer who was accused of supporting Trotsky. She was tried in 1937 and spent 18 years imprisoned in a labour camp.
>
> They started to work on me again. I was put on the 'conveyor belt'. The interrogators worked in shifts. I didn't. Seven days without sleep or food. Relaxed and fresh, they passed before me as a dream. The object of the 'conveyor' is to wear out the nerves, weaken the body, break resistance, and force the prisoner to sign whatever is required. Others confessed for the sake of their families and some, most especially Bukharin, confessed as a last service to the Communist Party.

> **Source J** From Gregory Zinoviev's speech at the end of his trial (August, 1936)
>
> I would like to repeat that I am fully and utterly guilty. I am guilty of having been the organiser, second only to Trotsky, of that block whose chosen task was the killing of Stalin. I was the principal organiser of Kirov's assassination. The party saw where we were going, and warned us; Stalin warned us scores of times; but we did not heed these warnings. We entered into an alliance with Trotsky.

> **Source K** From *Eastern Approaches*, Fitzroy MacLean, published in 1951. MacLean was a British diplomat who observed the show trials
>
> The prisoners were charged with every possible crime including high treason, murder, spying and all sorts of sabotage. They were accused of plotting to wreck industry and agriculture, to assassinate Stalin and break up the Soviet Union. Some were accused of betraying the Soviet cause even before the Bolshevik Revolution of 1917. One after another, using the same words, they admitted their guilt. And yet what they said seemed to bear no relation to reality.

ACTIVITIES

1 What point is the cartoonist trying to get across in Source L? How does the cartoonist achieve this?

2 Study Source M. Suggest reasons why 'Bukharin, confessed as a last service to the Communist Party.'

3 Describe the key features of the show trials.

Practice question

How useful are Sources K and M for an enquiry into the treatment of prisoners in the show trials? Explain your answer, using Sources K and M and your knowledge of the historical context. (*For guidance, see pages 85–87.*)

9.5 The consequences of the purges

The show trials were crucial for Stalin. They enabled him to remove – openly – well-known Bolsheviks and any potential rivals to his leadership. By the time of the last major show trial in 1938, Stalin had no credible opponent who could challenge his position – he was the last remaining Bolshevik from the 1917 Revolution (Trotsky had been exiled and had no powerbase in the Soviet Union and he was eventually murdered by one of Stalin's agents in 1940.)

Although the show trials and the purges enabled Stalin to secure total control over the Soviet Union, the human cost was enormous: millions were killed, and whole sections of society were terrorised into following the demands of the Soviet leader. It is impossible to know exactly how many were killed or imprisoned, however, in 1988 the KGB – the name for the secret police at that time – allowed some NKVD files to be examined. This revealed the figures shown in Table 9.1.

▼ **Table 9.1** Victims of the purges, 1937–38

Fate	Number of people
Executed	1 million
Died in labour camps	2 million
In prison, late 1938	1 million
In labour camps, late 1938	8 million

The removal of so many people in the years 1936–38 also became known as the Great Terror. There was great disruption as a result, not least in the army, where thousands of officers were removed, including its senior figures. This almost led to defeat against Germany in 1941–42 when Hitler's armies invaded. The purges also undermined much of Stalin's earlier work on building up industry (see pages 106–08). Able scientists, administrators and engineers were arrested, executed or imprisoned, which affected the quality of what was being produced.

Every part of Russia was affected. No village, no home, not even Stalin's own family could escape. His cousins and in-laws were victims of the **Red Terror** (Great Terror). Anyone could receive a knock on the door in the middle of the night and be dragged away by the secret police. No one felt secure. Some people took advantage to denounce neighbours or workmates in order to get their jobs. All trust disappeared. Eventually, the secret police had files on half the urban population in the Soviet Union.

Many were unfairly expelled from the Communist Party. This often had cruel consequences. Without the Party card, it was impossible to get a job. This punished the whole family. When both parents of one 13-year-old girl were arrested she was forced to live on the streets. In order to survive she had to tell the Young Pioneers (see page 93) that her parents were spies and deserved to be shot.

> **Source N** Osip Mandelstam, a poet who was arrested in 1934, on the effects of the purges
>
> Everybody seemed intent on his daily round and went smilingly about the business of carrying out his instructions. It was essential to smile – if you didn't it meant you were afraid or discontented. This nobody could afford to admit – if you were afraid, you must have a bad conscience. Everyone had to strut around wearing a cheerful expression as though to say: 'What's going on is no concern of mine. I have important work to do and I'm terribly busy. I am trying to do my best for the State, so do not get in my way.'

◀ **Source O** A mass grave at Cheliabinsk, 1938 Why do you think that the bodies were buried in mass graves?

ACTIVITY

Using a concept map, show the effects of the purges and explain any links between them. You may wish to use the following categories – military, political, economic, social and psychological.

Practice questions

1 Give two things you can infer from Source N about the effects of the purges. (*For guidance, see page 77.*)
2 Explain why there was little opposition to the purges.

> You may use the following in your answer:
> ■ Secret police
> ■ Patriotism
>
> You must also use information of your own.

(*For guidance, see pages 95–96.*)

9.6 The utility question

This section provides guidance on how to answer the question about utility.

In answering the utility question, you must analyse various aspects of two sources and, in order to reach the top level, you need to cover them all. The content and the nature, origin and purpose (NOP) of a source should be considered and out of this there will emerge an evaluation of the source's utility and reliability. In addition, you must also include knowledge of the historical context to support inferences and/or to assess the usefulness of information.

In order to reach higher level marks for this question you have to explain the value (usefulness) of both the content and the NOP of each source. The NOP is found in the provenance of the source – the information given above or below it. A good tip is to highlight or underline key words in the provenance which show either the utility or the limitations of the source. An example of this approach is given for Source A on page 86.

There is also guidance in the box below about what to consider for the NOP of a source.

NOP MEANS ...

N Nature of the source

What type of source is it? A speech, a photograph, a cartoon, a letter, an extract from a diary? How will the nature of the source affects its utility? For example, a private letter is often very useful because the person who wrote it generally gives their honest views.

O Origins of the source

Who wrote or produced the source? Are their views worth knowing? Are they giving a one-sided view? When was it produced? It could be an eyewitness account. What are the advantages and disadvantages of eyewitness accounts?

P Purpose of the source

For what reason was the source produced? For example, the purpose of adverts is to make you buy the products; people usually make speeches to get your support. How will this affect the utility of the source?

Question 1

How useful is Source A for an enquiry into the murder of Kirov? Explain your answer, using Source A and your knowledge of the historical context.

How to answer

Although in the exam the question will be on two sources, in Question 1 we look at one source to help you build your skills in analysing a source. Question 2 on page 86 is about the utility of two sources.

First let us concentrate on content. For each source you should think about the following questions:

1 What is **useful** about the content of the source?
   - What does it mention? How useful is this compared to your own knowledge of the event? This is known as your contextual knowledge.
   - What view does it give about the feelings of people? Can you add any contextual knowledge to support your answer?

For example:

> Source A states that Zinoviev admitted guilt for the murder of Kirov. It is useful because the death of Kirov was, and still is, a mystery and this links Kirov's mysterious death to Trotsky. This is useful as it supports the idea that Stalin wanted to discredit as many of his own opponents as possible – especially Trotsky – and that the show trials were a way of doing this. The trial was also a way of shifting the blame away from Stalin.

Now we will move on to NOP.

Page 86 shows examples of the values and limitations of the NOP of Source A as evidence of the show trials.

Nature

It is useful because it is from a speech in the show trial of the time and shows blame for Kirov's death. It is from a trial and should have some truth, but the show trials were a sham despite being made public. It is not that useful because Zinoviev was under pressure to confess and it is more than likely that he confessed in the hope that his family would not be harmed.

Source A From Gregory Zinoviev's, speech at the end of his trial in August, 1936

I would like to repeat that I am fully and utterly guilty. I am guilty of having been the organiser, second only to Trotsky, of that block whose chosen task was the killing of Stalin. I was the principal organiser of Kirov's assassination. The party saw where we were going, and warned us; Stalin warned us scores of times; but we did not heed these warnings. We entered into an alliance with Trotsky.

Origins

It is useful because it is from the actual trial and someone who knew Trotsky but its usefulness must be questioned because Stalin sought to remove his opponents by any means necessary.

Purpose

The speech is useful because it was made to the public and broadcast. It was to show that Stalin had found the murderers of Kirov and that there were enemies of the State and Stalin in high places. It is also useful because it shows how knowledgeable Stalin was and how he was able to see threats to the country. But the real purpose was for all of this to emerge from the mouth of an enemy. It is very useful because it shows Stalin's way of thinking and how he was able to get rid of his enemies. However, it is clear that the content of the speech is not reliable because it is made with Zinoviev experiencing threats to his family. Moreover, many knew that Zinoviev and Stalin had been at loggerheads over economic policy in the 1920s. Making Zinoviev speak at the end of the trial meant Stalin could also appear innocent of any involvement in the death of Kirov.

ACTIVITY ?

Now, have a go answering Question 1 using all the guidance given on pages 85–86. Make a copy of the planning grid below and use it to plan your answer. Include the value of the content of the source and any contextual knowledge to support that. Try also to add some contextual knowledge when you make a point in the NOP columns.

Contents	Value	Contextual knowledge
What does the source tell you?		
What view does the source give?		
NOP		
Nature		
Origin		
Purpose		

The utility of two sources

For this paper you will need to evaluate the utility of two sources.

Question 2

How useful are Sources B and C for an enquiry into the show trials? Explain your answer, using Sources B and C and your knowledge of the historical context.

> **Source B** Fitzroy MacLean, a British diplomat who observed the show trials
>
> The prisoners were charged with every possible crime including high treason, murder, spying and all sorts of sabotage. They were accused of plotting to wreck industry and agriculture, to assassinate Stalin and break up the Soviet Union. Some were accused of betraying the Soviet cause even before the Bolshevik Revolution of 1917. One after another, using the same words, they admitted their guilt. And yet what they said seemed to bear no relation to reality.

> **Source C** From *The Trial of the Seventeen* by Leon Trotsky, a newspaper article published in 1937
>
> How could these old Bolsheviks who went through the jails and exiles of Tsarism, who were the heroes of the civil war, the leaders of industry, the builders of the party, diplomats, turn out at the moment of 'the complete victory of socialism' to be saboteurs, allies of fascism, organizers of espionage, agents of capitalist restoration? Who can believe such accusations? How can anyone be made to believe them? And why is Stalin compelled to tie up the fate of his personal rule with these monstrous, impossible, nightmarish judicial trials?

How to answer

- Explain the value of the contents of each source and try to add some contextual knowledge when you make a point.
- Explain the value of the NOP of each source and try to add some contextual knowledge when you make a point.

Make a copy of the following grid to plan your answer for each source, and use the writing frame below.

Source B	Value	Contextual knowledge
Nature		
Origins		
Purpose		
Contents		

> Source B is useful because it suggests (contents) ....
>
> This is supported by my contextual knowledge ....
>
> Moreover Source B is also useful because of (NOP) ....
>
> This is supported by my contextual knowledge...
>
> Source C is useful because it suggests (contents) ....
>
> This is supported by my contextual knowledge ....
>
> Moreover Source C is also useful because of (NOP) ....
>
> This is supported by my contextual knowledge ....

When Stalin became leader of the Soviet Union, he was aware that in order to secure his position, he needed to control every aspect of daily life. Collectivisation and the Five-Year Plans (see Chapters 11 and 12) were crucial to his aims, as were the purges, but he also realised that he needed the mass support of the people too. He ensured that propaganda was used extensively to put over the ideas of the government. Soviet citizens would be bombarded with Communist and Stalinist propaganda in all aspects of daily life and propaganda ran through all aspects of culture and education. Importantly, as in any totalitarian state, no alternative viewpoint was permissible in Stalin's Russia. All non-communist ideas were censored. Moreover, the campaign to glorify Stalin grew tremendously in the 1930s and was known as the 'cult of Stalin.'

10.1 The cult of Stalin

One of the key features of any totalitarian state is to glorify the leader and turn them into an almost god-like being. This 'cult of personality' was developed by Stalin, using the skills of propaganda he had developed as editor of *Pravda* (Truth).

To secure the support of the people, Stalin wanted all **Soviet** citizens – adults and children – to become aware of his own personal greatness. It became impossible to avoid seeing and hearing glowing references to Stalin. His name and picture were everywhere. Streets and cities were named after him and poems and plays were written about him. Newspapers constantly carried stories of his wonderful achievements and they gave him nicknames such as 'Man of Steel', 'Shining Sun of Humanity' or *Vozhd* (the Boss). He created the image of himself as a caring leader (see Source A) whose genius had saved the Soviet Union from its enemies and made it the envy of the world. Huge parades in Red Square in Moscow, films, statues and paintings all showed how fortunate the Soviet people were to have such a great leader. For most Soviet citizens, Stalin became the 'Universal Genius'. His policies would create the New Soviet Man who would reject old Russia and embrace the only true **socialist** way – that is, the way of Stalin.

Artists, writers and film-makers were instructed to produce works in praise of Stalin and his achievements. Ordinary people were told that Stalin was the centre of all that was good and wise. He promised to reward those who were loyal to him with better housing and promotion at work. Party members, such as Avdienko in Source B, were forever praising his achievements.

▲ **Source A** Propaganda poster of Stalin from the 1930s

Source B From a speech by A. Avdienko, a writer, to the Congress of Soviets, February 1935

All thanks to thee, O great educator, Stalin. I love a young woman with a renewed love and shall perpetuate myself in my children – all thanks to thee, great educator, Stalin. I shall be eternally happy and joyous, all thanks to thee, O great educator, Stalin. Everything belongs to thee, chief of our great country. And when the woman I love presents me with a child the first word it shall say will be: Stalin.

Changing history

Stalin had to rewrite history to glorify his own part in the past, especially the **Bolshevik Revolution**, and remove the part played by 'enemies' such as Trotsky and other leading **Bolsheviks**. Photographs were doctored so that these people disappeared from Soviet history. In this way, images of Bukharin, Zinoviev and Kamenev were eventually removed from photographs.

At the same time, new paintings and histories were created, emphasising Stalin's role, especially his apparent close links with Lenin, who was still treated as a god in Soviet society (see Source C). Stalin even encouraged the 'cult of Lenin' but with himself close at hand. Photographs were faked to show Stalin close to Lenin (see Source D).

▲ **Source C** A patriotic painting showing Lenin directing the shelling of the Winter Palace during the 1917 revolution. The artist has placed Stalin in a prominent position among Lenin's aides

▲ **Source D** A fake photograph. Stalin (right) has been added to this photograph of Lenin, originally taken in 1922

ACTIVITIES

1 What image does Source A give of Stalin? How does the artist create this image?

2 What can you learn from Source B about what some people thought about Stalin? How is it helpful in enabling you to understand the adoration of Stalin?

3 Explain how Sources C and D help you understand why Stalin changed history.

4 You are a Soviet historian who has been asked to rewrite the Bolshevik Revolution of 1917 to greatly enhance the part played by Stalin.
   a) Look at pages 30–34 to see what actually happened.
   b) Now rewrite the events of October/November to show that Stalin played a key role.

Practice question

Explain why Stalin introduced the 'cult of personality'.

You may use the following in your answer:
■ Secure his position
■ Indoctrination

You must also use information of your own.

(For guidance see pages 95–96.)

10.2 Control of culture and religion

Stalin saw writers and artists as dangerous because they had the potential to criticise him and his work. Therefore, all writers' work was carefully censored. It had to be submitted to committees before it was published, as described in Source F. Any artists who deviated from the official Communist **Party line** were severely punished and many who fell foul of the Union were sent to the *gulag labour camps* in Siberia.

The Union of Soviet Writers was founded in 1932 to control the content of the work of authors to ensure it promoted an official culture and would act as propaganda for the state (see Source E).

> **Source E** From a speech by A. Zhdanov to the Union of Soviet Writers at its first Congress, 1934. Zhdanov was leader of the Union
>
> In our country the main heroes of works of literature are the active builders of a new life – working men and women, men and women collective farmers, Party members, business managers, engineers, members of the Young Communist League, Pioneers. Our literature ... is the spirit of heroic deeds. It is optimistic ... because it is the literature of the rising class of the proletariat ... Our Soviet literature is strong by virtue of the fact that it is serving a new cause – the cause of socialist construction.

> **Source F** From Victor Serge's *Memoirs of a Revolutionary*, 1945
>
> Censorship, in many forms, mutilated or murdered books. Before sending a manuscript to the publisher, an author would assemble his friends, read his work to them and discuss together whether such-and-such pages would 'pass'. The head of the publishing group would then consult the Gavlit, or Literature Office, which censored manuscripts and proofs.

Media censorship

Stalin ensured that the people of the Soviet Union had little knowledge of the outside world. Culture was closely controlled (see above) and the press was subject to stringent controls. The main communist newspapers were *Pravda* (Truth) and *Izvestiya* (News). There were jokes in the 1930s in the Soviet Union that there was no truth in *Pravda* and no news in *Izvestiya*.

Papers linked to communist organisations were heavily censored and local and regional newspapers were also subject to **censorship**. Radio was closely controlled and foreign radio stations were jammed.

Socialist realism

Writers, artists, film-makers and even composers had to support the government by following the policy of '**socialist realism**'. Artists belonged to the Russian Association of Proletarian Artists and writers belonged to the Russian Association of Proletarian Writers (RAPP). RAPP ensured that members did not deviate from the proletarian line – class struggle had to be the focus of any new writing. (RAPP was re-named the Union of Soviet Writers in 1932.) Writers such as Valentin Kataev wrote about workers building new cities such as Magnitogorsk. Soviet films had to be straightforward and designed for the masses. Music, art, poetry and plays had to be intelligible to the ordinary person and anything abstract was frowned upon. Art had to be about real working people or show the struggle to move to a better life in a socialist state. Great composers such as Shostakovich and Prokofiev were ordered to write only music that all could understand. This meant that many of the new artistic developments of the early twentieth century could not be reflected in Soviet culture.

The result was that artists' work had to deal with ordinary people, and had to show how communism was developing. Above all, it had to give simple, clear and optimistic messages. Large statues of peasants and workers appeared across the Soviet Union showing harmony between groups of citizens (see Source G). All aspects of culture would show the successes of communism and there had to be no doubt that the Soviet Union was a happy, fulfilling country for its citizens. By the end of the 1930s, Soviet culture promoted Stalin's cult of personality and also nationalism because of the threat of war. The film *Alexander Nevsky*, directed by Sergei Eisenstein in 1938, was a huge success because it portrayed Russian patriotism in the face of a German attack.

▲ **Source G** A sculpture by Vera Mukhina, 1937. The title of the work is 'A worker and a woman collective farmer'. The statue shows the man with a hammer as a symbol of industry and the woman with a sickle, a symbol of agriculture. This was designed to symbolise how the Soviet Union was changing

Religion

Religious groups posed a threat to the 'cult of Stalin' as they owed their allegiance to a different god. There were three main religious groups that Stalin had to deal with – Russian Orthodox, Muslim and Jewish – and Stalin continued and extended the Bolshevik attack on religion.

- Christian leaders were imprisoned. In the early 1920s, there were about 60,000 Russian Orthodox priests and only about 5,600 by the beginning of the war in 1941.
- Many churches were turned into museums.
- During the **Five-Year Plans** (see page 107), priests were driven from their villages and church bells were melted down to help industrialisation.
- More than 60,000 places of worship were closed down and during the **purges**, people worshipped in secret.
- 'The League of Militant Atheists' or 'Society of the Godless' was set up to promote anti-religious propaganda. Members smashed churches and burned religious pictures.
- Mosques and Muslim schools were closed and pilgrimages to Mecca were banned. Islamic law was banned and women were encouraged to unveil.
- Jewish schools, libraries and synagogues were closed down. The study of Hebrew was banned.
- No churches were allowed to be built in the new towns and cities.

However, despite these measures, it is thought that in the 1937 census, about 50 million Soviet citizens said they had religious beliefs. Some churches were permitted to remain open in the late 1930s – and by allowing this, Stalin could say that the idea of 'freedom of conscience' contained in the 1936 **Constitution** (see page 94) was being followed.

After the war began in 1941, Stalin allowed religious worship again in order to foster unity in the nation in the face of the German invasion.

▲ **Source H** A poster against the Church published in 1932 entitled 'The Kingdom of the Church – A Kingdom in Chains'

Practice question

Give two things you can infer from Source F about censorship under Stalin. (*For guidance, see page 77.*)

ACTIVITIES

1 Study Source E. Suggest reasons why some writers did not wish to follow the ideas of the Union of Soviet Writers.

2 In what ways does Source G. help you understand social realist forms of art?

3 What message does Source H give about the Orthodox Church?

4 Explain why Stalin controlled religion in the Soviet Union.

10.3 Control of education

In 1932 a rigid programme of education was introduced. The Bolsheviks had made many changes to the education system (see page 69), which had not brought the progress they expected. Stalin returned to more traditional methods. Discipline was strict (see Source I) and examinations were brought back. There were even fees in some of the advanced secondary schools.

This widespread propaganda campaign of an official culture was directed particularly at children. Children were taught that Stalin was the 'Great Leader'. They learnt Stalin's version of history. He even had a new book, *A Short History of the USSR*, written for school students, which showed him playing a more important role in the **revolution**. The teaching of communist **ideology** became compulsory in schools and, in addition, Stalin chose the subjects and information that children should learn. 'Red specialists' often replaced teachers who were not Communist Party members.

> **Source I** Rule One of the Twenty Rules of Behaviour. Pupils had to learn these rules by heart
>
> It is the duty of each school child to acquire knowledge persistently so as to become an educated and cultured citizen and to be of the greatest possible service to his country.

> **Source J** From the memoirs of Nadezhda Mandelstam, written in 1971. She was a poet whose husband, Osip, was purged and died in a prison camp
>
> Varia showed us her school textbooks where the portraits of the Communist Party leaders had thick pieces of paper pasted over them as one by one they fell into disgrace. The children had to do this on the instructions of their teacher.

„МЫ ТРЕБУЕМ ВСЕОБЩЕГО ОБЯЗАТЕЛЬНОГО ОБУЧЕНИЯ"

◀ **Source K** A Soviet propaganda poster from 1930. The caption says 'We insist on the total obligatory education'

Successes

Education changed to focus on the technical and scientific skills needed by Soviet workers who were involved in the Five-Year Plans (see page 107). Stalin did not wish to rely too long on foreign technicians. Indeed, by 1939, 94 per cent of urban dwellers and 86 per cent of the rural population were able to read and write. Furthermore, the Soviet Union was producing a high number of engineers, teachers, doctors and scientists.

> **Source L** A Russian official describes educational progress in Russia by 1938
>
> During the twenty-one years of the existence of the Soviet Union this aspect of the country has undergone a radical change. A formerly backward and poverty-stricken country has now become an enlightened, cultured and strong socialist power. Half the population are studying in elementary, secondary and higher schools. Illiteracy has now been completely obliterated. In the school year of 1914–15 there were only 155,000 children between the ages of eight and eleven years in the schools of Georgia. Now there are 658,000 such school children.

Youth groups

Outside school, Stalin also wanted some control over the young. Children joined political youth groups, which trained them in socialism and communism. The youth groups were taught activities such as sports, camping and model-making, and there were different groups for different ages:

- 8 to 10-year-olds joined the Octobrists
- 10 to 16-year-olds joined the Young Pioneers (see Source M)
- 16 to 28-year-olds joined the *Komsomol* (see Source N).

> **Source M** The promise made by each member of the Young Pioneers
>
> I, a Young Pioneer of the Soviet Union, in the presence of my comrades, solemnly promise to love my Soviet motherland passionately, and to live, learn and struggle as the great Lenin bade us and the Communist Party teaches us.

▲ **Source N** 1933 A recruiting poster for *Komsomol*. The caption says 'Prepare for worthy successors to the Leninist *Komsomol*'

ACTIVITIES ?

1 Study Source J. What was the purpose of forcing schoolchildren to paste over the photographs of disgraced Soviet leaders?

2 Explain the effects on education of the changes introduced by Stalin.

3 Can you trust what this Soviet official has written in Source L? Explain your answer.

4 What image do Sources M and N give of the Young Pioneers and the *Komsomol*?

Practice questions

1 Give two things you can infer from Source I about what was expected of schoolchildren in the Soviet Union? (*For guidance, see page 77.*)

2 Explain why was it important for Stalin to control everyday life of Soviet citizens?

You may use the following in your answer:
- Education
- Culture

You must also use information of your own.

(*For guidance, see pages 95–96.*)

10.4 The new constitution of 1936

In 1936, Stalin introduced a new **constitution**. This was to convince Soviet citizens and the outside world that the USSR was a 'free' society. In fact, it merely served to confirm Stalin's dictatorship. The USSR was now composed of 11 **socialist republics**. The old Congress of the Soviets of the USSR became the **Supreme Soviet** or parliament of the USSR, with two chambers – the Soviet of the Union and the Soviet of Nationalities (see Figure 10.1).

The Communist Party kept close control of both the central government and the government of each republic. Stalin held the posts of Prime Minister in the government, General Secretary of the Party and Chairman of the Party's **Politburo**.

The Constitution also set out some basic ideas about life in the Soviet Union (see Source O).

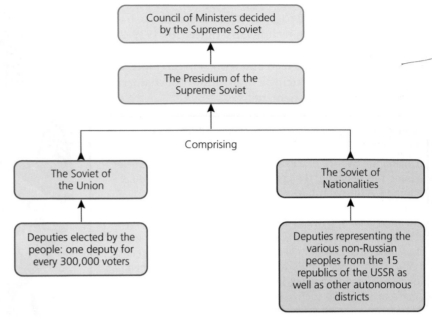

▲ **Figure 10.1** The Government of the Soviet Union (based on the 1936 Constitution)

Key features of the constitution

Stalin described the constitution as 'the most democratic in the world'. Its key features were:

- secret ballots
- elections to the soviets every four years
- candidates for elections had to be approved by the Communist Party
- universal suffrage (voting rights) for all over the age of 18
- guaranteed civil liberties, such as freedom of speech, press, assembly, religion and freedom from arbitrary arrest.

However, the Constitution made it clear that the freedoms were to be exercised only with the approval of the Communist Party. Moreover, the Communist Party was the only party permitted to exist within the USSR. In elections, the Party candidate would be the only candidate and sometimes the results were announced before voting took place.

Despite the claims made by Stalin about the new constitution, real power lay with the Communist Party. There were no elections for bodies in the Communist Party – members were chosen. The two most important parts were the Politburo and the **Central Committees**, but these did not always meet on a regular basis and Stalin made all decisions with his group of close advisers.

Source O Article 12 of the 1936 constitution

In the USSR work is a duty and a matter of honour for every able-bodied citizen in accordance with the principle 'He who does not work, neither shall he eat.' The principle applied in the USSR is that of socialism – 'From each according to his ability, to each according to his work.'

Practice question

Give two things you can infer from Source N about the idea of work in the Soviet Union. *(For guidance, see page 77.)*

ACTIVITIES

1 Explain why Stalin introduced the constitution in 1936.

2 Was the constitution democratic? Complete the table below, using the details on this page.

Democratic	Undemocratic

10.5 Causation question

This section provides guidance on how to answer the causation question. Look at the question below:

Question 1

Explain why Stalin introduced measures to control religion.

You may use the following in your answer:
- Cult of personality
- Different religions

You **must** also use information of your own.

How to answer

- Ensure you do not simply describe the two given points.
- Focus on the key words in the question, for example the theme of the question, which is causation, and any dates.
- Make use of at least the two given points and one of your own, or develop at least three points of your own.
- Write one good length paragraph on each point, fully explaining each.

The diagram on page 96 shows the steps you should take to write a good answer to this question. Use the steps and examples to complete an answer to the question by writing paragraphs on each point (your own and those given) and linking them where possible. Alternatively you could use the flowchart below to structure your answer to the question.

INTRODUCTION
- Explain the key theme of the question.
- Suggest the key areas you are going to cover in your answer.

FIRST PARAGRAPH – FIRST GIVEN REASON (OR REASON OF YOUR OWN)
- Introduce the first reason.
- Fully explain this reason.

SECOND PARAGRAPH – SECOND GIVEN REASON (OR REASON OF YOUR OWN)

THIRD PARAGRAPH – REASON OF YOUR OWN (OR GIVEN REASON IF NOT YET COVERED)

Step 1
Write an introduction that identifies the key reasons you need to cover in your answer and your main argument.

Example
Stalin wished to control all aspects of life and religion played a very crucial role in almost all citizens' life. If he was to win over everyone and control their thoughts, then religion was a key area. He needed to remove the importance of the three main religions so that he had no competitors or challengers. The communist state was also against religion as a philosophy.

Step 2
Write at least one good length paragraph for each of at least three reasons.
For each paragraph:
• Introduce the reason (green in the example).
• Fully explain it (blue in the example).

Example
The first reason was that Stalin wanted no competitors or challengers to him as leader of the Soviet Union, therefore he removed people such as Trotsky and then moved to challenge religion. Developing the cult of personality was a clever way of challenging religion because his actions were all positive. He presented himself as all-knowing and all-powerful and to do so he could have no religion which looked up to a god. Therefore, images of him were seen everywhere and he was given names such as 'Shining Sun of Humanity' which seemed to show him as a living god. Towns, cities, streets were named after him and his measures won support from many people and justified his measures in controlling religion.

Step 3
Now do the same for the second reason.

Example
A further reason was to spread his control over everyday life of people. He imprisoned priests and Church leaders (Christian, Jewish, Muslim) so that the faiths could not operate properly. Churches were closed down and religious items were removed to prevent possible future use. Stalin prevented Muslims going on the pilgrimage to Mecca and Islamic law was banned. Jewish synagogues were closed down. These attacks meant he was controlling everyday life and opponents could and would be removed.

Step 4
Write one more paragraph on another reason.

Example
A final reason was to show people how the communist state was against religion as a philosophy. Stalin even set up societies such as the League of Militant Atheists to put over his message about his dislike and distrust of religion. The Bolsheviks had always mistrusted organised religion and Stalin's methods not only reduced its importance but also drove worshippers underground. His policies meant that he was able to control yet another part of life across the Soviet Union.

Question 2

Explain why there were changes to the lives of young people under Stalin's leadership in the years 1928–41.

You may use the following in your answer:
■ Stalin's ideas
■ Education

You **must** also use information of your own.

ACTIVITY ?

Now have a go answering Question 2 using the steps shown for Question 1.

Economic and social changes, 1924–41

This key topic examines the period from the death of Lenin to the involvement of the Soviet Union in the Second World War. It examines why there were changes in industry and agriculture and how those changes affected the lives of Soviet citizens. It also analyses the successes and failures of the industrial and agricultural policies and assesses the human cost. In addition, it considers the impact on specific groups such as women and ethnic minorities.

Each chapter within this key topic explains a key issues and examines important lines of enquiry as outlined below.

CHAPTER 11 AGRICULTURE AND COLLECTIVISATION

- Stalin's reasons for changes in agriculture.
- The organisation of the collectives, mechanisation, widespread opposition and attach on the *kulak*s. Famine in the Ukraine.
- The successes and failures of collectivisation.

CHAPTER 12 CHANGES IN INDUSTRY

- Stalin's motives for rapid industrialisation, including the failings of the NEP.
- *Gosplan*, the Five-Year Plans and the Stakhanovite Movement.
- The successes and failures of industrialisation.

CHAPTER 13 LIFE IN THE SOVIET UNION

- Living and working conditions and the differing experiences of social groups.
- Changes in family life and employment and the political position of women.
- Reasons for, and features of, the persecution of ethnic minorities.

TIMELINE

1928	Collectivisation begins. Start of the first Five-Year Plan. End of the NEP	1934	About 7 million *kulak*s had perished in the process of collectivisation
1929	Pace of collectivisation increases	1935	Start of Stakhanovite Movement
1932–33	Famine in the Soviet Union	1938	Start of the third Five-Year Plan
1932	Sixty per cent of farms collectivised	1940	240,000 *kolkhoz* established
1933	Start of the second Five-Year Plan		

11 Agriculture and collectivisation

Stalin spent four years of political manoeuvring to become sole leader of the Soviet Union. When he became leader in 1928, he was then able to carry out the policies which he thought would not only create a communist state but also enable him to secure and maintain his position. Stalin was determined to modernise the Soviet economy. He introduced a series of Five-Year Plans that transformed industry and a policy of collectivisation, which brought major changes to agriculture.

11.1 Reasons for changes in agriculture

In some respects farming had not changed for hundreds of years and, before **collectivisation**, many farms still followed the medieval system of farming strips of land using horse-drawn wooden ploughs. Stalin introduced the policy of collectivisation in 1928 whereby peasants had to give up their own small plots of land in order to pool their land with those of other families (see Sources A and B). This would make a farm large enough to use modern machinery and the peasants would have to provide the state with a fixed amount of produce and earn a wage for doing so. Through using these methods, the idea was to create a surplus of food to feed the industrial workers in the towns (there was a grain shortage in 1928) and to sell abroad, and to use the profit made from the land to finance a programme of **industrialisation**. Stalin wanted to transform the USSR from a backward agricultural country into a modern industrial one (see Source C).

> **Source A** From a speech about problems in agriculture by Stalin to the Communist Party Congress in 1927
>
> What is the way out? The way out is to turn the small and scattered peasant farms into large united farms based on cultivation of the land in common … on the basis of a new higher technique. The way out is to unite the small and very small peasant farms gradually but surely, not by pressure but by example and persuasion into large farms based on common co-operative collective cultivation of the land.

> **Source B** A Communist Party official speaking to peasants about collectivisation, 1930
>
> Tell me. You wretched people, what hope is there for you if you remain on individual pieces of land? From year to year you divide and sub-divide your strips of land. You cannot even use machinery on your land because no machine could stand the rough ridges that the strip system creates. Don't you see that there is nothing ahead of you but ruin and starvation?

> **Source C** From a speech by Stalin in February 1931. He was talking about the backwardness of the Soviet Union
>
> We must create in our country an industry which would be capable of re-equipping and organising the whole of our industry but also our transport and agriculture. The history of Russia shows that because of her backwardness she was constantly defeated. Those that fall behind get beaten. No, we refuse to be beaten. We are 50 and 100 years behind the advanced countries. We must make good this distance in ten years. Either we do it, or we shall be crushed.

Stalin's rationale was based on a combination of economic and political factors that were linked by a fear of foreign invasion. He believed that if the Soviet Union was to compete with the industrialised nations of the world, then the only way to do this was by state intervention, which would also lead to greater control over the people of the Soviet Union – one of Stalin's key aims. He made it clear that workers would have to accept personal sacrifices in pursuit of these targets.

The main reasons for the modernisation of industry and agriculture are outlined under the headings below.

Fear of invasion

The help given by Britain, France and the USA to the **Whites** during the civil war of 1918–21 (see page 49) seemed to confirm Stalin's fears of an attack from the West. Modernisation of agriculture and industry was essential if the Soviet Union was to be sure of victory in any future war, as it would enable the armed forces to be built up and supplied. There were several war scares in the USSR in the late 1920s and there was a growing feeling of **diplomatic isolation** among many leading politicians. The modernisation of industry and agriculture would strengthen the country and, they hoped, deter any would-be opponent.

Disappointing output

Soviet industrial production remained disappointingly low. Stalin felt that central direction and control would enable him to direct the economy and ensure a rapid expansion in heavy industry in order to outstrip the developed nations. Agriculture under the NEP (see page 66) had failed to produce enough to feed Soviet industrial workers and therefore Stalin felt that state control was needed.

Communist principles

Stalin also had political reasons to modernise Soviet agriculture and industry. Collectivisation fitted in with communist ideas of common ownership. In 1925, as a result of the New Economic Policy (see pages 65–67), less than one per cent of the land was collectivised. By creating and sharing wealth among the Soviet people he hoped to create a strong state based on communist principles, where the state controlled economic activity. Stalin thought that the NEP was allowing the farmers (*kulaks*) to make large profits and he did not want this to continue.

Leadership

Introducing collectivisation would consolidate Stalin's push for leadership of the Soviet Union. The right-wing members of the Communist Party's Politburo – Bukharin, Tomsky and Rykov (see page 73) – were in favour of keeping the New Economic Policy. The launching of collectivisation would enable Stalin to discredit and remove these leading figures. If they could be removed as a result of the debate over agricultural policy, then he would strengthen his position as leader of the Party.

Control of the people

As well as wanting to modernise the Soviet Union, Stalin also sought to control the people, especially the peasants, by means of collectivisation. This would give Stalin control over the countryside and the peasantry, something that Lenin had failed to achieve. Stalin did not trust the peasants. He saw them as natural enemies of communism and he was aware of how close they had come to destroying Lenin during the time of War Communism (see pages 61–63). He believed that by taking away the peasants' independence he could remove any threat from them once and for all.

Industrialisation

If the Five-Year Plans were to be successful, agriculture had to produce surpluses that would be sold abroad and finance the initial stages of the Five-Year Plans. (The Five-Year Plans were Stalin's strategy for changing the Soviet Union to a highly industrialised country that could compete with the major powers of the world. These plans are examined in more detail in Chapter 12.)

Mechanisation was crucial, because it would release large numbers of peasants to work in the towns and cities.

There would be fewer farm workers in the countryside. The remaining ones would have to produce enough for the growing urban population. They also had to produce enough food to sell abroad (see Table 11.1) to bring in foreign currency to allow investment in materials for new factories. Sometimes there was insufficient food for the whole population. It was a difficult problem for Stalin to solve – unless some sections of society were allowed to starve.

▼ **Table 11.1** Soviet government figures of grain exports 1929–32 in millions of tonnes

Date	Millions of tonnes of grain exported
1929	0.18
1930	4.76
1931	5.06
1932	1.73

The problems of the NEP

Before collectivisation, Soviet peasants used old-fashioned, inefficient farming methods. Agriculture was still based on small peasant plots with little use of machinery. Even under the New Economic Policy, farmers were not producing enough food for the workers in the cities. After 1926, the amount of surplus grain given to the government by the peasants had been falling. The peasants had become wary of growing too much food, knowing it would be seized by the state at a low price.

The grain crisis of 1927–8

There was a war scare in 1927 and, as a result, some of the peasants began to hoard grain. Stalin saw this as an attempt to force up the price of grain and sabotage the work of the Bolsheviks. Stalin was keen to ensure adequate supplies for workers in the cities and therefore stated that *kulaks* had to produce specific quotas of grain for 1928. The *kulaks* reduced production because they would not receive as much money. Though the grain crisis was short-lived, it convinced Stalin that the *kulaks* would have to be controlled in the future and the best way to do this was by collectivising agriculture.

ACTIVITY

Explain the reasons why Stalin introduced collectivisation.

Practice questions

1 Give two things you can infer from Source C about Stalin's attitude to modernising the Soviet Union. (*For guidance, see page 77.*)
2 How useful are Sources B and C for an enquiry into why collectivisation was introduced? (*For guidance, see pages 85–87.*)

The attack on the *kulak*s

There was increasing pressure from some Bolsheviks to remove the wealthier peasants (the *kulak*s) who had become richer during the New Economic Policy – they were accused of being capitalists and hoarding food for their own consumption, rather than providing it for industrial workers in the towns. Collectivisation would get rid of them as a class.

Source D Extracts from speeches made about collectivisation by Stalin in 1928 and 1929

Look at the *kulak* farms: their barns and sheds are crammed with grain. They are waiting for prices to rise. So long as there are *kulak*s there will be sabotage of our grain needs. The effect will be that our towns and industrial centres, as well as the Red Army, will be threatened with hunger. We cannot allow that. We must break the resistance of this class and deprive it of its existence.

Source E From a speech by Stalin to the Communist Party of the Soviet Union in 1929. Here he was threatening the *kulak*s

We must eliminate the *kulak*s as a class. We must smash the *kulak*s ... we must strike at the *kulak*s so hard as to prevent them from rising to their feet again. We must annihilate them as a social class.

▲ **Source F** Soviet poster of a peasant working on his own plot of land rather than in the collective

ACTIVITIES

1 How effective do you think Source F would be in turning the Soviet people against the *kulak*s? Why was it displayed across the Soviet Union? Give reasons for your answer.

2 Study Sources D, E and F. Explain why Stalin was keen to focus on the *kulak*s as enemies of the state.
   a) Create a concept map of the reasons behind Stalin's decision to modernise agriculture on pages 98–100.
   b) Add links between the reasons on your diagram
   c) Explain which you think is the most important reason.

Practice question

Explain why the grain crisis of 1927–28 was important for Stalin.

You may use the following in your answer:
■ Control of the *kulak*s
■ Feeding the workers in cities

You must also use information of your own.

(For guidance, see pages 95–96.)

11.2 The organisation of collective farms

Collectivisation was supposed to be undertaken on a voluntary basis, but within a year it was being imposed on the peasants. Anyone who opposed the process was labelled as a *kulak* and an enemy of the state, and deported to Siberia and the Urals.

Kolkhoz

The Russian word for a **collective farm** is *kolkhoz* and it replaced the *mir* or village **commune**.

Local Communist Party officials went into villages and explained how the collective farm or *kolkhoz* would be organised. The most important figure in the *kolkhoz* was the chairman, who was a Communist Party member, usually from the nearest town. Once established, the *kolkhoz* would then claim ownership of animals, grain supplies and buildings in the village.

By 1940, there were about 240,000 *kolkhoz*. They were normally made up of 80 or so peasant families who farmed around 500 hectares of land. The families had to provide a fixed amount of food for the state at very low prices and peasants received a small wage. The peasants could keep any surplus. Members of the *kolkhoz* also had their own private plots of land.

Mechanisation of farming was developed. The state provided each collective farm with machinery, especially a tractor, other tools and seeds. In addition, Machine Tractor Stations (MTS) were set up. There was normally one of these for every 40 collective farms. Tractors and drivers from the MTS moved between the collectives to carry out the ploughing. By 1933, there were some 2900 MTS, which controlled more than 120,000 tractors. Members of the secret police were employed in some of the first MTS. This was another means by which Stalin was able to gain political control over the peasants.

> **ACTIVITY** ?
>
> Explain the effects of collectivisation on Soviet agriculture.

▲ **Source G** Peasants on a collective farm in the 1930s, learning about the benefits of the changes to agriculture

▲ **Source H** A mid-twentieth century Soviet painting of life in a *kolkhoz*

Sovkhoz

There was also a type of farm called a *sovkhoz*, which was usually created from the old, large estates. In the *sovkhoz*, all land was owned by the state and all produce was taken by the state. The *sovkhoz* was usually about 3,600 hectares and, unlike the *kolkhoz*, had its own tractors. The peasants worked as paid labourers and were referred to as workers. One historian has called the *sovkhoz* 'a factory without a roof'.

ACTIVITIES ❓

1 Describe the key features of a *kolkhoz* using the information on page 101 and Source H.

2 Study Sources G (on page 101) and H. In what ways are these sources helpful to you in understanding collectivisation?

11.3 Opposition to collectivisation

There was fierce opposition to collectivisation, especially in the agricultural areas of the Ukraine and Caucasus. Many peasants set fire to their farms and slaughtered their animals, rather than hand them over to the state (see Source I). The scale of the slaughter was staggering – from a total of 60 million cows, 30 million were killed, and 16 million horses died out of a total of 34 million.

Stalin retaliated by sending in de-kulakisation squads – Party members from the towns and the **OGPU** – to round up opponents of his policy, as explained in Source J. It is impossible to find an accurate figure, but possibly as many as ten million people were deported in the war against the *kulaks*.

> **Source I** From *Virgin Soil Upturned*, a novel by M. Sholokov, 1934. Sholokov lived in the Soviet Union during the period of collectivisation
>
> Both those who had joined the *kolkhoz* and individual farmers killed their stock. Bulls, sheep, pigs and even cows were slaughtered. The dogs began to drag entrails around the village; cellars and barns were full of meat. Young and old suffered from stomach ache. At dinner times tables groaned under boiled and roasted meat.

> **Source J** From *I Chose Freedom* by Victor Kravchenko, published in 1947. He witnessed collectivisation and the attack on the *kulaks* in one village. Kravchenko was a high-ranking Soviet official in the 1930s who eventually sought political asylum in the USA
>
> A number of women were weeping hysterically and calling the names of their fathers and husbands. In the background, guarded by the OGPU and soldiers with drawn revolvers, stood about twenty peasants, young and old, with bundles on their backs. A few were weeping. The others stood there sad and helpless. So this was 'liquidation of the *kulaks* as a class'. A lot of simple peasants being torn from their native soil, stripped of all their worldly goods and shipped to some distant labour camps.

Impact of opposition

The extent of opposition forced Stalin to slow down the process of collectivisation in 1930. Indeed, he blamed over-keen Party officials for the problems in carrying out his policy and, during the spring and summer of that year, there was some reversal of the process. He also made some concessions, including allowing members of the collectives to have some animals and a small garden plot for their own use. However, in late 1930, collectivisation began again. By 1932, 62 per cent of peasant households had been collectivised, and five years later the number had increased to 93 per cent.

ACTIVITIES

1 What were the immediate effects of collectivisation?
2 Explain why the *kulaks* were so opposed to collectivisation.

Practice question

Give two things you can infer from Source J about the impact of collectivisation on the *kulaks*. (*For guidance, see page 77.*)

11.4 The successes and failures of collectivisation

1 HUMAN COST

The human cost of collectivisation was enormous. There was a serious famine from 1932 to 1933, which caused the death of somewhere between six and ten million peasants (see Sources K–N). In the Ukraine and the northern Caucasus about five million people died.

2 BENEFITS

The aim of producing enough food to feed the towns and the Red Army was achieved. Life on the collective farms was not all bad. For example, there were schools and hospitals on some collectives for the workers. The MTS (see page 101) were quite successful and the mechanisation of farming did speed up in the years after 1935. By 1936, more than 90 per cent of land had been collectivised and tractors were introduced on a large scale.

5 GREATER CONTROL

Collectivisation was also a success for Stalin and the communists. They had finally secured control of the countryside. The peasants never again openly rebelled against communist rule. Stalin had also ensured that he had a secure supply of food for the towns and workers for the factories.

Effects of collectivisation

3 FALL IN PRODUCTION

Economically, collectivisation had mixed results. Peasant opposition led to a serious decline in grain production, from 73.3 million tonnes in 1928 to 67.6 million in 1934 (see Table 11.2). The impact on the countryside was worsened by the government policy of seizing grain. The rural population starved in order to provide for the needs of industry, and peasants moved to the towns in search of food. Such movement was stopped when the government introduced passports simply for moving around the country. The peasants thus became tied to the collectives and were little better off than the serfs of tsarist Russia.

4 INEFFICIENT FARMING

Farming remained inefficient, with Soviet farmers producing less per head than farmers in the USA or western Europe. Until the mid-1930s, there was not enough food grown for the whole Soviet population and some had to be purchased from abroad. The worst years were 1932–33 when a national famine occurred. It was not until 1940 that figures for grain production matched those of 1914. Historians have found little evidence that collectivisation provided surplus food to sell abroad and the strategy therefore failed to provide adequate foreign capital for Stalin's investment programme.

▲ **Figure 11.1** The effects of collectivisation

Source K From an eye-witness account of the famine in the Ukraine, 1932

The poor widow, Darylul, and her sons, had a very tragic end. Her dead body was eaten by maggots and the two sons dropped dead begging for food … Oleska Voitsyskhovsky saved his and his family's lives by consuming the meat of horses which had died of disease. He dug them up at night and brought the meat home in a sack.

Source L Bystanders looking at a victim of the Ukraine famine (*Holomodor*), 1932

◄ **Source N** The *Holodomor* memorial in the Ukraine honours the millions of victims of the famine of 1932–33

▼ **Table 11.2** Consumption of foodstuffs (in kilos per head)*

Year	Bread	Potatoes	Meat	Lard/Butter
1928	250.4	141.11	24.8	1.35
1932	214.6	125.0	11.2	0.7

* The figures are Western estimates based on soviet statistics

▼ **Table 11.3** Comparative numbers of livestock (in millions) and grain production (in million tonnes), 1929–35*

	1929	1930	1931	1932	1933	1934	1935
Grain	71.7	83.5	69.5	69.6	68.4	67.6	75.0
Cattle	67.1	52.5	47.9	40.7	38.4	42.4	49.3
Pigs	20.4	13.6	14.4	11.6	12.1	17.4	22.6
Sheep/goats	147.0	108.8	77.7	52.1	50.2	51.9	61.1

* The figures are Western estimates based on soviet statistics

ACTIVITIES

1 What can you learn from Sources L and M about the effects of collectivisation?

2 Look at the effects of collectivisation (Figure 11.1).
  a) Organise the effects into successes and failures and set out your answer as a two-column table.
  b) Overall, do you think the successes outweigh the failures?

3 Study Table 11.2 and Table 11.3.
  a) What can you learn from the source about the impact of collectivisation on food production?
  b) Why do think that the table caption says 'Western estimates based on Soviet statistics'?

4 What does Source M mean? Explain your answer.

? Practice question

Explain why Stalin introduced collectivisation in 1928?

You may use the following in your answer.
- Control of the *kulaks*
- Industrialisation

You must also use information of your own.

(*For guidance, see pages 95–96.*)

12 Changes in industry

Stalin was determined to modernise Soviet industry as quickly as possible. For this reason he introduced a series of targets for industry known as the Five-Year Plans. These brought about rapid growth, especially of heavy industry, and provided employment opportunities for women (*crèches* were set up to help with childcare, for example). By 1941, Stalin had transformed the country into the second strongest industrial nation in the world. However, this was achieved at a great human cost – often poor working and living conditions for workers and the use of slave labour from the *gulags*.

12.1 Stalin's motives for rapid industrialisation

In the years after 1928 Stalin introduced a series of **Five-Year Plans**. These plans set production targets for **Soviet** industry. Workers in each industry were told exactly how much they must produce. Stalin believed that the Five-Year Plans were the only way to transform the Soviet Union into an industrial power in a short space of time; his response to those who said that the pace of **industrialisation** was too fast was '... those who lag behind are beaten ...'.

He had many motives for introducing this rapid industrialisation. Firstly, he was convinced that surrounding **capitalist countries** would invade the Soviet Union. Only a strong industrial economy could produce the wealth and modern weapons that the Soviet Union needed if it was to survive such an attack.

Furthermore, if Stalin's plans to modernise agriculture were to be achieved, then industry had to change immediately. Changes in farming meant that the Soviet Union would need thousands of tractors and fuel to power them (see Source A).

In addition, Stalin strongly opposed the **New Economic Policy (NEP)** because it allowed private enterprise and went against the ideals of communism. He was determined to restore central or state direction of industry, which would in turn give him full control of Soviet industry. If he went ahead with the Five-Year Plans, it meant he would be able to out-manoeuvre Bukharin, Rykov and Tomsky (see pages 73–74).

▲ **Source A** A 1930 photograph of the first tractor produced at the Stalingrad Tractor Works

ACTIVITY ?

Study Source A. This was used as a propaganda poster. Devise a suitable caption for this photo.

Practice question

Explain why Stalin introduced the Five-Year Plans.

You may use the following in your answer:
- Fear of foreign invasion
- Control of industry

You must also use information of your own.

(For guidance see pages 95–96.)

12.2 The Five-Year Plans

In 1928, the NEP was abandoned and the first Five-Year Plan was launched. This was to be directed by *Gosplan* (the state planning authority), which set targets for certain key industries and ensured they were given priority in the allocation of manpower and raw materials.

The First Five-Year Plan, 1928–32

The first Five-Year Plan concentrated on heavy industry, such as coal, steel and iron. The 'new' industries, such as electricity, motor vehicles, chemicals and rubber, were also targeted but consumer industries, such as textiles and household goods, were neglected.

New industrial centres

When new factories and industrial centres were constructed, they were situated in eastern areas of the Soviet Union such as Kazakhstan, areas far away from any possible attack by the West (see Figure 12.1). Huge towns and industrial centres were built from scratch deep inside the USSR (see Source B). For example, Magnitogorsk concentrated on iron and steel. Little had existed there before the Five-Year Plan and workers were either encouraged or forced to move to the site. In the space of three years, 1929–32, Magnitogorsk grew from 25 to 250,000 people.

▲ **Source B** *Komsomol* volunteers at a construction site in the new city of Komsomolsk, Siberia in the 1930s

ACTIVITIES ?

1 What can you learn from Figure 12.1 about the location of industry during the Five-Year Plans?

2 Study Source B. Why would this be used for propaganda purposes?

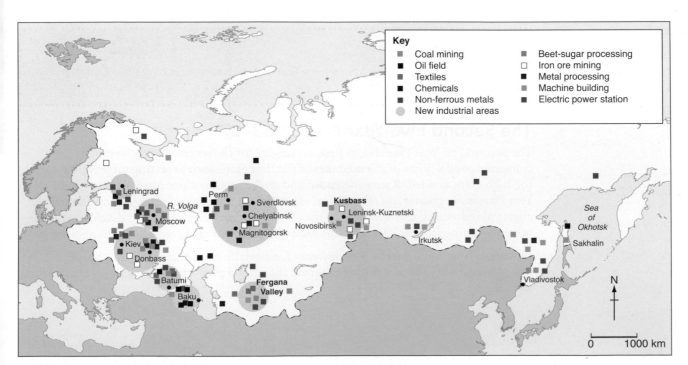

Key
- Coal mining
- Oil field
- Textiles
- Chemicals
- Non-ferrous metals
- New industrial areas
- Beet-sugar processing
- Iron ore mining
- Metal processing
- Machine building
- Electric power station

▲ **Figure 12.1** Location of different industries during the Five-Year Plans

Impact of the plan

Workers were expected to work as hard as possible in order to reach the targets that Stalin set. If individual workers did not meet targets, then they were shamed publicly in the factory or workplace. Some could not cope with the pressure and there was an increase in **absenteeism**. This then led to checks being made on the workers, and those who did not have convincing reasons for their absence could find themselves being sent to work on forced labour projects in Siberia.

Yet, despite the hard work, terrible conditions and eventual food rationing, most people were enthusiastic about the Five-Year Plans. There was a feeling that a new country was being created and that **socialism** would bring a better society to the Soviet Union. Thousands of Soviet citizens, especially young people, volunteered to go to the east and build new industrial centres such as Magnitogorsk.

Stalin was encouraged by the apparent success of the plan and he revised the targets twice – Table 12.1 shows the original and revised targets alongside the actual figures.

▼ **Table 12.1** Industrial output during the first Five-Year Plan

Production (in million tonnes)	1927–28 Original targets	1932–33 'optimal' (highest expected)	1932 revised targets	1932 actual output
Coal	35.0	75.0	95–105	64.0
Oil	11.7	21.7	40–55	21.4
Iron Ore	6.7	20.2	23–32	12.1
Pig Iron	3.2	10.0	15–16	6.2

Source C A report from the British Embassy to the British government, 21 June 1932. It was describing the First Five-Year Plan

It is a record of over-staffing, overplanning and complete incompetence at the centre. It is a record of human misery, starvation, death and disease among the peasantry. The only creatures which have any life at all in the districts visited are boars, pigs and other swine. Men, women, and children, horses and other workers are left to die in order that the Five-Year Plan shall at least succeed on paper.

Practice question

Give two things you can infer from Source C about the human cost of the first Five-Year Plan. *(For guidance, see page 77.)*

The Second Five-Year Plan, 1933–37

The Second Five-Year Plan did, at first, set targets for the increased production of consumer goods. Some of the mistakes of the first plan, such as setting targets that were too high, were avoided. Rationing ended and strikes were not permitted. The second Five-Year Plan made greater use of technical expertise, with spectacular growth in the coal and chemical industries, and successes in the output of electricity, transport development and mineral mining (copper, zinc and tin). However, oil production remained disappointing.

As fears of invasion from the West increased, especially from Nazi Germany, heavy industry again became the priority. During the second plan, the production of armaments trebled.

▲ **Source D** Alexei Stakhanov explaining his working methods to fellow miners

THE STAKHANOVITE MOVEMENT

The miner Alexei Stakhanov became a hero of the Soviet Union when, on the night of 30–31 August 1935, it was claimed that he shifted 102 tonnes of coal, which was almost 15 times the normal amount for a single shift. It was, however, a set-up. He had two helpers who removed the coal while he worked at the coalface with his pick. In the workplace, employees were urged to work harder through encouragement and the example of people such as Alexei Stakhanov (see Source E). The Stakhanovite Movement encouraged workers to follow Stakhanov's example and they formed 'shock brigades' in attempts to copy their worker hero.

The **Stakhanovites**, as they were known, were rewarded with medals (the 'Order of Lenin' or 'Hero of the Soviet Union'), new houses, free holidays and other benefits. However, the campaign was quietly dropped in the late 1930s after a number of Stakhanovites were beaten up and killed by their fellow workers.

The Third Five-Year Plan, 1938–41

The Third Five-Year Plan was launched in 1938, but was abandoned when Germany invaded the Soviet Union in June 1941. It concentrated on the production of household goods and luxury items, such as bicycles and radios, but then heavy industry became the main priority as war loomed ever closer. Though armaments were produced in great number, there were problems in the steel and oil industries. The third plan also experienced problems because of the **purges** (see page 78), as many senior workers and officials were removed. This resulted in a lack of continuity with the earlier plans.

ACTIVITIES

1 a) What was meant by the term 'Stakhanovite movement'?
   b) Why do you think Stalin considered the Stakhanovites to be so important?

2 Describe the key features of the Five-Year Plans, using the sources, tables and the information on pages 107–09.

3 Write a newspaper article about the Five-Year Plans, with the headline 'Stalin introduces revolutionary plans to modernise the Soviet Union'. In your article explain the effects of the Five-Year Plans on Soviet industry.

12.3 Successes and failures of industrialisation

Successes

Although the plans' targets were not all met, all Soviet industries made remarkable advances and, by 1940, the USSR was the world's second-largest industrial power behind the USA, with a highly skilled workforce.

Industrial production

The figures in Table 12.2 are drawn from the work of the economic historian E. Zaleki, whose findings are based on careful analysis of Soviet and Western sources. They give an overview of industrial production during the Five-Year Plans, showing how productivity increased. Interpretation 1 supports the idea that the plans were an overriding economic success.

▼ **Table 12.2** Industrial output during the Five-Year Plans

Production (in million tonnes)	1927	1930	1932	1935	1937	1940
Coal	35	60	64	100	128	150
Steel	3	5	6	13	18	18
Oil	12	17	21	24	26	26
Electricity	18	22	20	45	80	90

Interpretation 1 From a history of the USSR written by a Soviet historian in 1981

Whilst the economies of the capitalist states were sinking ever deeper into recession, the Soviet economy was booming. The second sections of the Magnitogorsk and Kuznetsk iron and steel complexes were completed ahead of schedule. At the start of the Five-Year Plan a major victory was scored on the industrialisation front when the Urals heavy engineering plants went into operation. Good progress was made in constructing new railways and motorways. During the second Five-Year Plan period, industrial output went up by 120 per cent.

ACTIVITIES

1 How far do you agree with Interpretation 1 about the success of the Five-Year Plans? Explain your answer.

2 Why was it important to have an educated workforce?

3 What image of life under Stalin is provided by the song in Source E? Pick out the key words or phrases which provide this image.

A skilled workforce

In 1929, Soviet workers lacked many of the skills needed to carry out industrialisation. The workforce was essentially illiterate, unskilled and undisciplined. The main problems facing managers in factories were drunkenness and absenteeism – many workers returned to their villages after they had failed to come to terms with the discipline of factory life.

Between 1929 and 1937, investment in education and training schemes created a skilled workforce. A new **elite** emerged – teachers, scientists, engineers, factory managers and skilled workers – who were paid far higher wages than ordinary workers. Like many officials, they also received extra benefits, such as better housing or the right to buy scarce foods. They enjoyed a higher standard of living, which went against communist principles, but Stalin realised that incentives had to be used in order to attract the right calibre of people.

Source E In 1934, Stalin announced in a speech that 'life was getting better'. Two years later the song 'Life's Getting Better' was written by Aleksandr Aleksandrov

Beautiful as birds all in a row

Songs fly above the Soviet land.

The happy refrain of the cities and fields:

'Life's getting better

And happier too!'

The country is growing and singing as one,

It forges everyone's joy with its songs.

Look at the sun—the sun's brighter too!

'Life's getting better

And happier too!'

There's room everywhere for our minds and our hands,

Wherever you go you'll find you have friends.

Old age feels warmer, and youth braver still—

'Life's getting better

And happier too!'

Know, Voroshilov, we're all standing guard—

We won't give the enemy even a yard.

There is a saying for folks old and young:

'Life's getting better

And happier too!'

Let's let the whole gigantic country

Shout to Stalin: 'Thank you, our man,

Live long, prosper, never fall ill!'

Development of cities

In the years 1929–39, the population of the USSR's cities rose by 29 million. Vast construction projects were undertaken, such as the Dnieper Dam hydroelectric power station, the Belomor Canal, the Moscow Metro underground (Source G) and the Moscow-Volga canal.

Failures

However, the targets of the Five-Year Plans were frequently too ambitious and set at unrealistic levels. As a result, some were not achieved. Officials at every level often gave false or exaggerated production figures in order to satisfy the demands of *Gosplan*. The production of textiles actually declined during the first Five-Year Plan and the housing industry was virtually ignored. Above all, there was a serious shortage of consumer goods.

Quality remained an over-riding problem in each of the plans. Many of the workers were peasants, with little experience of working with machines; for example, half the tractors produced for the **collective farms** soon broke down. Industry grew so rapidly that the shortage of skilled workers became a real problem, so much so that the first Five-Year Plan produced only 50,000 tractors, when the target was 170,000 (Source F).

Working conditions

Workers endured tough living and working conditions in order to achieve economic progress. Peasants were also pressed into working in the factories. They were not used to the harsh industrial regime and experienced terrible conditions, similar to the workers before the **Revolution**. Millions died as a result of Stalin's policies; and yet there were people who defended the vision Stalin put forward and believed that his policies meant a strong Soviet Union. Stalin stressed that the Soviet Union was under constant threat of invasion and that his policies were the only way to ensure security. Any person who complained about living and working conditions was to be considered an enemy of the state.

ACTIVITIES

1 Some workers were paid more than others. Write a letter of complaint to Stalin asking how this could be explained in a communist society.

2 a) Make your own balance sheet showing the successes and failures of industrialisation. Set it out as a two-column table.

   b) Overall, do you think the successes outweigh the failures? Give reasons for your answer.

3 What messages do Sources F and G give about the success of industrialisation?

▲ **Source F** Workers on the first tractors coming off the assembly line at the tractor works in Stalingrad, 1934

▲ **Source G** Soviet poster published in 1934 entitled 'All Moscow builds the Metro'

13 Life in the Soviet Union

Industrialisation, collectivisation and the purges brought rapid changes to the lives of people in the Soviet Union during the 1930s. The role of women, in particular, was transformed, although not necessarily for the better. Ethnic groups suffered more than most, especially from Stalin's policy of Terror, while living conditions for many worsened due to the demands of the Five-Year Plans.

13.1 Living and working conditions

Economic progress was often achieved at the expense of tough living and working conditions in towns.

Working conditions in towns

Working conditions were harsh in cities and towns – there were strict rules about discipline and punctuality and very high productivity demands as a result of the Stakhanovite movement (see page 109). Many peasants were pressed into working in the factories. They were not used to the harsh industrial regime and experienced terrible conditions, similar to the workers before the revolution.

Fines were imposed for lateness and bad workmanship, and workers who were absent for more than a day were sacked. Failures were always blamed on **saboteurs** rather than on the system. The secret police encouraged workers to inform on one another. Anyone blamed for obstructing work could be sent to a labour camp or shot. For example, in 1928, 55 engineers working in the Shakhty coalmines in the Donbass were put on trial for sabotaging equipment and organising accidents. Despite their innocence, five were shot.

Moreover, workers were poorly paid. The value of their wages fell by 50 per cent, meaning that something they could buy in 1928 cost them twice as much in 1933. There was a great shortage of everyday goods, and there were few workmen to carry out domestic repairs. Crime, alcoholism and juvenile delinquency increased.

Strikes were not permitted and demands for higher pay and better working conditions were seen as acts of selfishness at a time when the survival of the USSR was threatened.

Forced labour

Some of the biggest projects in the **Five-Year Plans** were carried out in appalling conditions by forced labour – prisoners in *gulags*. Many of these workers were peasants who had opposed **collectivisation** (see page 103) and they built, among other projects, the Belomor Canal and the Moscow Metro. These conditions are described by an eyewitness in Source A.

> **Source A** An eyewitness account of conditions during the building of the Belomor Canal in the 1930s
>
> At the end of the day there were corpses left on the worksite. Two were frozen back to back leaning against each other. At night sledges went out and collected them. In the summer, bones remained from corpses which had not been removed in time.

▲ **Source B** Construction of the Belomor Canal by *gulag* prisoners in 1932

> ### Practice question
>
> Give two things you can infer from Source A about working conditions during the building of the Belomor Canal. *(For guidance, see page 77.)*

Living conditions in the towns

There is much debate over the living conditions in towns and cities during **industrialisation**. As shown in the diagram below, there were some improvements, but, for many, conditions were very poor.

FAMILY BENEFITS

There were several benefits brought in for families. For example, there was a free health service for all, holidays with pay for many workers and an insurance scheme against accidents. Women and girls who had just left school found it easy to secure employment and this meant there was less pressure to recruit workers from rural areas.

NO UNEMPLOYMENT

Soviet workers did not experience an economic depression, unlike countries such as Britain, Germany and the USA where millions were out of work.

URBAN LIVING CONDITIONS

Many towns and cities found it difficult to cope with the rapid population growth. Roads, water supply, power and transport often could not cope. Moscow, the capital city, was the exception. Some places had no bathhouses for entire populations and others had no sewage systems. Many towns had no street lights and it was dangerous to venture out late at night.

BETTER CONDITIONS

WORSE CONDITIONS

LEISURE

Sport and exercise were encouraged to improve the general fitness of Soviet men and women. Trade unions and collective farms provided clubs, sports facilities, film shows and general entertainment.

OVERCROWDING

The urban population rose from 29 million in 1929 to 40 million only four years later and this increase continued throughout the 1930s. It proved impossible to build enough new houses for the millions of peasants who flooded into the towns and cities or worked in the new industrial centres, and pressure increased on all the basic amenities – trams and buses never had enough space. Most families had to live in overcrowded and run-down buildings, such as those described in Source C, and share flats with several other families. Often there was one family per room and they had to share the bathroom and kitchen. In Moscow, only 6 per cent of households had more than one room.

Source C A description of a Moscow apartment by Freda Utley, from her memoirs *Lost Illusion*, 1949. Utley was an American Marxist who lived in the Soviet Union during the 1930s

Badly built, with doors and windows of unseasoned wood, which could not be shut properly. Unpapered and thinly whitewashed walls, these two rooms were home. By American and British standards, we were living in a squalid tenement house. But by **Soviet** Russian standards we were housed almost as Communist aristocrats. We not only had two rooms to live in. We had the luxury of gas for cooking. Best of all we had a bathroom with a lavatory, which we had to share with only one other family.

Living and working conditions in the countryside

Living and working conditions for peasants in the countryside were heavily impacted by Stalin's policy of collectivisation (see page 101). For some it brought benefits, but many were worse off.

Better conditions

Following collectivisation, there was greater **mechanisation** which made work and life much easier for the peasants. Some of the drudgery was removed and the use of tractors speeded up work. The collectives brought in scientists who worked alongside the farmers. These scientists introduced new ideas and new methods in order to bring the farmers into the twentieth century. Moreover, at the beginning of collectivisation, peasants were offered free housing to join collectives and even seed to begin cultivating crops.

Some collectives had schools and literacy rates improved during the 1930s. Collectives also had hospitals – it was vital that there was a healthy workforce to produce the food for the urban workers. The farm workers had the same social benefits as the workers in cities.

Worse conditions

However, many peasants resented collectivisation. They thought the **Bolshevik Revolution** had been about giving them more freedom and land, but instead, under Stalin, they had to give up their land and livestock to the collective farm. Any opposition was met with fierce treatment. So much so that Stalin introduced forced collectivisation and confiscated any land that the peasants and *kulaks* had. Within a few years, Stalin had destroyed a system of farming that had existed for several hundred years.

Peasants who remained in the collectives eventually found it difficult to move to the cities because they had to have a passport to do so. This tied the peasants to their collective, making them like serfs of the nineteenth century. The Machine Tractor Stations had members of the secret police on their staff and were able to keep an eye on the members of the collectives.

An important part of peasants' life was taken away as their churches were destroyed or closed down. In some places these closures caused riots.

In addition, there were often food shortages (see page 104) because the food that was produced was taken to feed the workers in the cities and towns.

◄ **Source D** A painting by a Soviet artist in the mid-1930s. It shows the peasants on a collective farm celebrating the harvest

Source E From a speech by a brigadier (leader) of a collective farm made in 1938

We have more than 600 hectares. Of those, 123 are sown with cotton, 225 planted with wheat. Our vineyards cover 45 hectares. Our three lorries can hardly cope with the work. Our farmers have built 70 new houses for themselves during the last years. Look inside these houses and you will find rich carpets and musical instruments. Four times this year the whole farm went to the theatre, to concerts and to the cinema. Look at our happy children. They all go to school. We have two schools. I could say much more about the life of our collective farm, but the young wine is bubbling impatiently in your glasses. Drink to the good Stalin, who brought us this life.

Practice question

How useful are Sources C (page 113) and D for an enquiry into living and working conditions in the Soviet Union during the Five-Year Plans? Explain your answer, using Sources C and D and your own knowledge. (*For guidance, see pages 85–87.*)

ACTIVITIES

1 Work in pairs. You are reporters who are interviewing two different families in Moscow in the mid-1930s, one that has benefited from life under Stalin and one that has not. Write out your questions and answers.

2 Source D was a propaganda poster. Devise a suitable caption that could have been used for this poster.

3 Who do you think was better off under Stalin, town workers or peasants? Copy the table below and collect evidence for your answer from the information and sources on pages 112–14. Then write a paragraph explaining your answer and supporting it with the evidence you have collected.

	Better off	Worse off
Town worker		
Peasant		

13.2 The differing experiences of social groups

Stalin's principal aim was to remove anyone considered to be a class enemy of socialism, especially Nepmen, *kulaks* and anyone who had capitalist tendencies. The proletariat was to rule supreme over the Soviet Union.

Party members

Stalin was determined to encourage peasants and members of the proletariat to become members of the Communist Party and to rise to prominent positions. He wanted a career ladder for the new elite of the Party. This was successful, because it produced future leaders such as Khrushchev and Brezhnev. Moreover, the higher up the ladder you moved, the better your lifestyle. This could include better housing, better healthcare and even a villa, known as a *dacha*, for holidays in the countryside (see Sources F and G).

The peasants

Collectivisation and the purges removed the wealthier peasants, the *kulaks* (see page 100). However, conditions for the mass of the peasantry were worse than those of town workers. The state kept the price of agricultural produce low to ensure a cheap supply of food for the towns. As a result, at the beginning of the collectivisation process, more and more peasants moved to the towns to find work and, they hoped, a better standard of living.

The town workers

Stalin was also keen to encourage movement to higher positions in industry. Workers were promoted into management jobs. For example, over 1.5 million workers gained management posts under the First Five-Year Plan. Some workers also benefited from the expansion of higher education which enabled them to gain the technical knowledge needed for higher management posts. In addition, the rapid industrialisation caused by the Five-Year Plans removed unemployment completely.

The down side was that the huge increase in the urban population led to poor living conditions. Furthermore, as we have seen, working conditions were harsh. Some peasants did not move to the towns because of the strict rules and high demands on productivity (see page 112).

Source F From *Everyday Stalinism*, Sheila Fitzpatrick, published in 2000

The leaders of the soviet in the city of Kazan undertook to build a whole settlement of *dachas*, using as was later alleged, money improperly diverted from other parts of the area budget (transport, sewage and parks) and also with other funds for local 'bigwigs'.

ACTIVITY ?

1 Describe the experiences of different social groups in the Soviet Union in the years 1928–41.

2 Party members experienced a better quality of life than others, especially as they moved higher up. How might this not match up with the idea of a communist society?

▼ **Source G** Stalin's *dacha* in Sochi on the Black Sea coast. It was built in 1937

13.3 The changing position of women

When the **Bolsheviks** took over in 1917, they immediately passed a decree, which stated that women were equal to men. Lenin wanted to emancipate women from their traditional role in the home. In order to do this, the Bolsheviks understood that there would have to be more *crèches* and nurseries and that divorce and abortion would have to be made easier. However, there were no revolutionary changes for women in the 1920s. Men still clung to the traditional view of the domestic role of women (even if they had full-time jobs) and the Bolshevik Party did not always practice what it preached about equality. The idea of state *creches* and kindergartens was cast aside when the cost would be too great.

Education did change for women and in 1929, 20 per cent of places in higher education were reserved for women. Places for engineering and in the sciences showed the greatest increases. By 1940, 40 per cent of engineering students were female.

◀ **Source H** Soviet girls learning to read in a state-run literacy class in the 1930s

Family life

By the mid-1920s, the Soviet Union had the highest divorce rate in Europe. In 1927, two thirds of marriages ended in divorce. However, by the mid-1930s, the family was back in favour and divorce and abortion were more difficult to obtain. The high divorce rate of the 1920s and early 1930s had created a great number of broken homes and homeless children who lived on the streets begging and robbing. Through propaganda, such as the article in Source I, the state tried to encourage families to stay together – for example, by paying child allowances for married couples, making divorce much harder and restricting abortion.

> **Source I** An extract from an article in *Pravda* in 1936
>
> When we talk of strengthening the Soviet family we mean to fight against wrong attitudes towards marriage, women and children. 'Free love' and a disorderly sex life have nothing in common with Socialist principles or the normal behaviour of a Soviet citizen. The outstanding citizens of our country, the best of Soviet youth, are almost always devoted to their families.

Employment

Women did make some progress in the sphere of employment. They were encouraged to work in almost all areas. Some women took on jobs like engineering, which had once been done only by men. However, life remained hard for most Soviet women. They were expected to work full time, as well as bring up a family. State nurseries and *crèches* provided help. Women were encouraged to work to help achieve the Five-Year Plans – the number of female workers in towns rose from 3 million in 1928 to 13 million in 1940. Facilities such as *crèches* were provided to help women continue working after childbirth. There were some improvements in education and health for the workers and their families. All workers' children received free primary education and free healthcare schemes were extended to cover most of the workforce.

> ### Practice question
>
> Give two things you can infer from Source I about changes to family life in the Soviet Union in the mid-1930s. (*For guidance, see page 77.*)

Political position

Politically, women still remained second-class citizens. By 1928, only 12.8 per cent of the party members were women. Very few women rose to high positions in the Party or government. There was a women's department in the Bolshevik Party (*Zhenotdel*) which was founded by two female revolutionaries – Alexandra Kollontai and Inessa Armand. *Zhenotdel* organised for women in factories to be elected as delegates so that they could participate more in politics. As a delegate, the elected women would spend time as observers in various branches of public activity such as factories, soviets, trade union organisations, schools and hospitals. They would then report back to the Zhenotdel and explain where the revolution was not being followed.

The Zhenotdel published women's pages in national and local party newspapers and all women were encouraged to send reports to the press. There were conferences and congresses for women throughout the 1920s.

The Zhenotdel was abolished in 1930 as part of party 'reorganisation', when it was declared that women's issues had been solved and that any future issues among women would become the work of the party as a whole.

Trotsky said that 'to change the conditions of life you have to learn to see them through the eyes of a woman' and after 1930, he said women were being returned to the 'old slavery'.

The Communist Party remained male dominated and there was no further push to allow women into positions of real power under Stalin.

▲ **Source J** Painting of a female construction worker, 1937

▲ **Source K** Government poster of the 1930s. The slogan reads 'The wide development of a network of *crèches*, kindergartens, canteens and laundries will ensure the participation of women in Socialist reconstruction'

Practice question

Explain why Stalin's government made changes to the position of women in the Soviet Union in the years 1928–41.

You may use the following in your answer:
- Industrialisation
- High divorce rate

You must also use information of your own.

(For guidance, see pages 95–96.)

ACTIVITIES

1 Why do you think that many of the propaganda photographs about industrial change, such as Source J, featured women?

2 Study Source K. What message is the government trying to get across in this poster?

3 Draw a table like the one below and complete it using the information on women from pages 116–17. Use the evidence you collect to write a paragraph explaining whether you think there was more or less progress in the position of women during the 1930s.

Progress	Lack of progress

13.4 The persecution of ethnic groups

Stalin was faced with a dilemma as leader. According to the 1926 census, there were 176 nationalities and 120 languages in the Soviet Union and it had been decided in the Revolution that each nationality had a right to an education in its own language. Stalin wanted a united country but had to accept the various **socialist republics** which made up the Soviet Union. He wanted to use the Russian language and customs as the links to bind the union together. If there were groups who did not wish to be part of the Union, then he would deal with them accordingly. He did not want multiple national identities in the Soviet Union and hence, measures were taken to produce a country with a single language and culture.

Although Stalin was from the non-Russian state of Georgia, he had no sympathy for the plight of the many non-Russian groups that had suffered **persecution** and '**Russification**' under the tsars. Indeed, they experienced a particularly difficult time in the 1930s. Stalin distrusted **national groups**, which he believed might be disloyal to the regime. His aim was to turn these into 'Soviet citizens' rather than Ukrainians or Georgians. They were discouraged from speaking their own languages and practising their own customs and traditions. Russian became compulsory in schools and key jobs went to Russians. They were often discriminated against, with few having top positions in the army or government. Army recruits were sent away from their homelands and forced to mix with other ethnic groups. Many who opposed this were purged.

Deportation and purges

Government in Moscow was strengthened and the powers of the republics were reduced so that any nationalist tendencies were diminished. Any national groups which continued to threaten Stalin's policy were deported. Seven ethnic groups were deported from their native territories en masse: the Volga Germans; the Kalmyks; the Crimean Tatars; and the Chechens, Ingush, Karachai and Balkars of the Northern Caucasus. It has been estimated that more than 1.25 million people were moved and many of these died during their forced transportation.

▲ **Source L** Crimean Tatars waiting to be deported, 1930s

The Ukraine

Many Ukrainians were starved deliberately during the famine of 1932–33 (see page 104) because it was feared that many were seeking separation from the Soviet Union and Stalin wanted to remove this threat. In addition, Stalin purged many of the leading Ukrainian intellectuals who were thought to be encouraging separation. More than 5,000 Ukrainian intellectuals were arrested and later were either murdered or deported to prison camps in Siberia. These individuals were falsely accused of plotting an armed rebellion. However it was very clear that Stalin's intentions were to eliminate the leaders of Ukrainian society.

Border regions

From 1935 onwards, the Soviet government kept increasing 'cleansing' operations in border regions. Finnish, Latvian and Estonian families were deported from the Leningrad region to Kazakhstan and Siberia. At the same time, families of Polish and German origin were deported from the border district of Kiev.

Korean community

However, the largest single deportation took place in 1936 when the entire Korean community, some 172,000 individuals, was moved from the Vladivostok and Birobidzhan regions by the **NKVD** (see Source N). It took 124 railway convoys to move them to Uzbekistan and Kazakhstan. This was justified on the grounds that the Korean population was 'a breeding ground for spies for the Japanese secret service'.

Source M From Maya Lykashtarnaya, whose father, Todar, was born in Belarus. He was arrested in 1937 and sent to a labour camp, where he subsequently died

My mother hoped up to the very end, until they told her that he was sentenced to 10 years in jail without right of correspondence. This essentially meant that the person was no longer alive. This verdict was used when people were to be executed: sent away for 10 years, to some unspecified destination, without right of correspondence. My mother and myself also spent several years in a labour camp.

Source N From an interview with Roman Shin, whose Korean parents were forcibly deported in 1936

These Korean people were deported without being asked anything, in cattle trains. My parents were also deported. People were sent to Kazakhstan, to the steppe, or to Uzbekistan. A number died on the way or when they arrived. Stalin claimed they were acting as spies for the government of Japan.

ACTIVITIES

1 What does Source N suggest about the treatment of minorities in the Soviet Union?

2 Explain how ethnic minorities were treated in the Soviet Union in the years 1928–41.

3 Suggest reasons why Stalin was prepared to force thousands of Soviet citizens to move to other parts of the country.

Practice question

How useful are Source M and Source N for an enquiry into the treatment of ethnic minorities in the Soviet Union? Explain your answer, using Sources M and N and your knowledge of the historical context. (*For guidance, see pages 85–87*).

13.5 Further examination practice on interpretations

Here is an opportunity to practise answering some more interpretation questions.

▲ **Source A** The city of Magnitogorsk in the mid-1930s, which became an important centre for the iron and steel industry

Source B From a letter written in the mid-1930s and preserved in the Magnitogorsk archives. It is from Anna Kovaleva to Marfa Gidzia

We are both wives of locomotive drivers of rail transport in Magnitogorsk. You probably know that the railway workers of the MMK (Magnitogorsk Metallurgical Complex) are disrupting the supply of blast furnaces, open hearths and rolling shops. All the workers accuse our husbands. Every day there are stoppages and breakdowns in rail transport. I ask you, Marfa, to talk to your husband and persuade him to work conscientiously.

Interpretation 1 From *Stalin and Khrushchev the USSR, 1924–64* by M. Lynch, published in 1990

The Second Five-Year Plan was more realistic than the First Plan. Nevertheless, over-production occurred in some parts of the economy, under-production in others, with the frequent result that whole branches of industry were held up for lack of essential supplies. There was competition between regions and industries to obtain an adequate supply of essential supplies with considerable hoarding of resources. This led to a lack of co-operation necessary for integrated industrial growth. Complaints about poor standards continued to be made.

Interpretation 2 From *Russia and the USSR 1905–1956* by J. Shuter, published in 1996

In just ten years, the Soviet Union became the second largest industrial power in the world. Huge new steel plants, hydro-electric power stations, railways and canals were built. Vast numbers of factories in hundreds of new towns poured out manufactured goods. Between 1928 and 1932, the tiny village of Magnitogorsk in the Urals became an industrial city of over 250,000 citizens. This happened all over the Soviet Union.

Question 1

Study Interpretations 1 and 2. They give two views about the achievements of Stalin's Five-Year Plans. What is the main difference between the views? Explain your answer, using details from both interpretations.

> You need to give the views of each interpretation and back these up with evidence from each one.

Question 2

Suggest **one** reason why Interpretations 1 and 2 give different views about the achievements of Stalin's Five-Year Plans. You may use Sources A and B to help explain your answer.

> The interpretations may differ because:
> - they have given weight to two different sources. You can use evidence from Sources A and B for this answer. Match the sources to the interpretations
> - they are partial extracts
> - the authors have a different emphasis.

Question 3

How far do you agree with Interpretation 2 about the achievements of Stalin's Five-Year Plans? Explain your answer, using both interpretations and your knowledge of the historical context.

> You need to give a balanced answer which agrees and disagrees with the interpretation using evidence from the two interpretations as well as your own knowledge.
> - State the view given in Interpretation 2 using evidence from the Interpretation itself.
> - Agree with the view given in Interpretation 2 using your own knowledge.
> - Disagree with the view given in Interpretation 2 using evidence from Interpretation 1
> - Disagree with the view given in Interpretation 2 using your own knowledge.
> - Make a final judgment on the view given in Interpretation 2.

Revise and practise

1 Russia in early 1917

In under 25 words explain why each of the following were discontent in Russia at the start of the 20th century:

- Town workers
- Peasants
- Subject nationalities

2 The February Revolution

1 Draw a series of concentric circles. Place the following effects of the First World War on Russia in rank order, beginning with the most important in the centre of the circle to the least important on the outside. Give a brief explanation of your choice of the most important.
   - Inflation
   - Food shortages
   - Influence of Rasputin
   - Military defeat

2 Pair each of the following lettered sentences with one of the numbered sentences below:

   a) More and more peasants were called up to fight in the armed forces.

   b) Russia suffered defeat after defeat during the first year of the war.

   c) The tsar's frequent absences from Petrograd left the tsarina in charge of the government.

   d) Russia did not have a transport system that could cope with the demands of war.

   e) There were serious shortages of consumer goods such as boots and clothes.

   i) She was greatly influenced by Rasputin.

   ii) Vital supplies of food often failed to reach towns and cities.

   iii) Therefore Tsar Nicholas II decided to take over the command of the armed forces.

   iv) These shortages led to a rise in prices.

   v) This led to less land being ploughed and serious food shortages.

3 The Provisional Government

1 True or false:
   - The Provisional Government ended Russian involvement in the First World War
   - The Kornilov Revolt was defeated due to the support of the Bolsheviks
   - The Russia offensive of 1917 was a success
   - The July Days strengthened the Bolsheviks

   - Kerensky became the leading figure in the Provisional Government
   - There were increased food rations under the Provisional Government

2 Place the following events in chronological order:
   - The Kornilov Revolt
   - Trotsky becomes Chairman of the Military Revolutionary Committee
   - The Bolshevik seizure of power
   - Lenin's return from exile

4 The Bolshevik Revolution

Place the following events in chronological order:

- The Kornilov Revolt
- The Bolshevik seizure of power
- Trotsky becomes Chairman of the Military Revolutionary Committee
- Lenin's return from exile

5 Early consolidation of power, 1917–18

For the following two statements, write two or three sentences agreeing with them.

1 The Treaty of Brest-Litovsk was popular in Russia.

2 There was strong opposition in Russia to the Treaty of Brest-Litovsk.

6 The Civil War, 1918–21

Explain why each of the following was important in the civil war in the years 1918–21:

- Trotsky's train
- Admiral Kolchak
- The *Cheka*
- Foreign support for the Whites
- General Deniken

7 Changes under the Bolsheviks

1 Draw a table with four columns headed 'Why introduced', 'Key features', 'Successes' and 'Failures'. In less than five words, per column, summarise the differences between War Communism and the NEP.

2 Which of the these best sums up the NEP? Explain your choice.
   - It was an economic necessity but politically unpopular.
   - It was a political necessity but economically unpopular.

8 The struggle for power, 1924–28

1 What explanation can you give for the following contradictory statements?
   - Trotsky was the favourite to succeed Lenin and yet it was Stalin who became leader.
   - Lenin warned against Stalin as leader in his Testament and yet Stalin became leader.
2 Make a copy of the table and match the following statements to either Trotsky or Stalin.

Strengths of Stalin	Weaknesses of Trotsky

- He was too arrogant
- He had a key position as General Secretary of the Party
- He missed Lenin's funeral
- He was unpopular because he had been a Menshevik
- He was the Chief mourner at Lenin's funeral
- He underestimated his chief opponent
- He promised 'Socialism in One Country'
- He wanted world revolution
- He placed supporters in leading positions in the Party

9 The use of terror in the 1930s

1 Use illustrations to show the meaning of the following words/phases:
   - The purges
   - Murder of Kirov
   - Secret police
   - Labour camps
   - Show Trials
2 Which of the following are causes of, and which are effects of, the purges?

The murder of Kirov
The armed forces lacked leadership
Millions were sent to labour camps
Stalin's fear of the old Bolsheviks
Stalin had a persecution complex
Slave labour was needed for industrialisation
Stalin needed someone to blame for the failure of his policies
All the old Bolsheviks were eliminated
Even the Secret Police was purged

10 Propaganda, censorship and the cult of Stalin

Explain in two sentences how the following enabled Stalin to keep control of the Soviet Union:
- Culture
- The Constitution of 1936
- Education
- The cult of Stalin

11 Agriculture and collectivisation

Categorise the importance of the effects of collectivisation on the Soviet Union in the years 1928–41 by placing them in a series of concentric circles, beginning with the most important in the centre to the least important on the outside:
- Gave Stalin control of the peasants
- Got rid of the *kulaks*
- Led to famine
- Brought increased mechanisation

12 Changes in industry

1 True or false

	True	False
The First Five-Year Plan lasted four years		
The First Five-Year Plan concentrated on consumer goods		
Much industry was now located in the east		
The Third Five Year-Plan was interrupted by the German invasion of the Soviet Union		
Fines were introduced for lateness and absenteeism		
The Stakhanovites were popular with their fellow workers		

2 Match the definitions to the words
   a) Stakhanovites   b) *Gosplan*   c) Magnitogorsk
   d) Shock brigades   e) *gulags*
- State Planning Authority which set targets
- Workers who exceeded their productivity targets
- Groups of Stakhanovites
- Labour camps
- New industrial town

13 Life in the Soviet Union

1 Make a copy of the following grid. Summarise the key changes for each of the following.
   - Women
   - Ethnic minorities
   - Peasants
   - Workers
2 The following account of life under Stalin is by a student who has not revised thoroughly enough. Re-write the account, correcting any errors.

Less and less women worked in industry under Stalin. However, more and more women got top jobs in the Communist Party. At first divorce and abortion were easy. Later, they were both made more difficult. Stalin supported the rights of the ethnic minorities because he was from the Ukraine.

Glossary

Absenteeism   Unscheduled employee absences from the workplace

All-Russian Congress of Soviets   A meeting of representatives from the newly created soviets

Amnesty   An official pardon for people who have been convicted of political offences

Aristocracy   The highest social class including the people who have special titles such as duke and duchess

Armistice   A formal agreement of warring parties to stop fighting

Arsenals   A collection of weapons and military equipment

Autocracy   Rule by one person who has complete power

Bolshevik   A member of one of the groups formed after the split in the Social Democratic Party in 1903. The Bolsheviks (meaning 'majority'), led by Lenin, believed in a small party of dedicated revolutionaries

Bolshevik Revolution   This took place in October/November 1917 when the Bolsheviks seized power

Cabinet   A group of the leading ministers in the government

Cadets   The Constitutional Democratic Party which wanted a democratic style of government

Capitalism   Economic system based on private ownership of the means of production, distribution and exchange

Capitalist countries   Countries such as the USA and Britain which followed a capitalist economic system

Censorship   Banning or cutting parts of a newspaper, book, film, etc., which the government does not like

Central Committee   The highest organisation in the Communist Party elected by Party members

Centralisation   Control concentrated in the hands of the government in Moscow

Cheka   Secret police set up under Lenin's Bolshevik government

Collective farm   A farm or group of farms managed and owned through the state

Collectivisation   Process introduced by Stalin whereby individuals' farms and land were put together and then run by a committee. All animals, tools and the produce of the farm were to be shared

Comintern   Short for 'Communist International' – international organisation based in Russia, formed to assist the growth of communism all over the world

Commissar   Term for government minister

Commissar of Nationalities   Minister or member of government responsible for non-Russians

Commune   A village organisation controlled by heads of families – it redistributed land and organised payment of taxes

Concentration camps   A place in which large numbers of people, especially political prisoners or members of persecuted minorities, are deliberately imprisoned in a relatively small area with inadequate facilities

Conscription   The compulsory enlistment of people into military service

Constituent Assembly   Assembly or parliament elected for the purpose of drafting a new constitution

Constitution   The system of rules by which a state is ruled

Constitutional monarch   A monarch who has limited powers and is answerable to an elected parliament

Cossacks   A group of military warriors loyal to the tsar, living in the area of the Ukraine

Council of People's Commissars   This was the central government or cabinet of ministers set up by Lenin to rule Russia after the October Revolution

Counter-revolutionary   A person who takes part in a revolution that tries to reverse the results of one that has just occurred

Crèches   A day care centre where adults take care of children in place of their parents

Czech Legion   A group of Czech prisoners-of-war who escaped and travelled up and down the Trans-Siberian railway attacking the Bolsheviks

Desertion   The act of leaving a military position without permission

Diplomatic isolation   Many governments around the world refused to send ambassadors to the USSR and cut off all contact

Elite   An exclusive group or section

Ethnic cleansing   The systematic forced removal of ethnic or religious groups from a given territory by a more powerful ethnic group

Five-Year-Plan   Set of targets for industry laid down by the central planning organisation, *Gosplan*

Food requisitioning   The seizure of grain and other food supplies from the countryside by the Red Army and the *Cheka*

Garrisoned   (Of troops) stationed in a fortress or barracks

German Spring Offensive   The last major German attack on the Western Front in the First World War

Gosplan   The State Planning Authority, which set targets for industries and allocated resources. An organisation run by the Communist Party. It was given the task of planning the industrialisation of the USSR under the Five-Year Plans

Gulag   Prison where inmates were punished by forced labour

Haemophilia   Hereditary disease that prevents the blood from clotting during bleeding. Even a minor cut could lead to excessive bleeding and death

Ideology   The ideas that characterise a political system

Industrialisation   Process of developing key industries, especially heavy industries such as coal and iron

July Days   Refers to events in 1917 that took place in Petrograd, Russia, between 3 July and 7 July, when soldiers and industrial workers engaged in spontaneous armed demonstrations against the Russian Provisional Government

Komsomol   A youth organisation controlled by the Communist Party of the Soviet Union. The name comes from the first syllables of three Russian words meaning Communist Union of Youth

Kremlin   The twelfth-century citadel in the centre of Moscow containing the offices of the Soviet government

Kulak   The name given to the better-off peasants who had benefited from Lenin's New Economic Policy and who began to employ poorer peasants to work for them. Any rich farmer was called a *kulak*

Labour camps   A camp where inmates were made to engage in very hard and forced work

Left-wing   Refers to those who support more extreme radical views such as socialism and communism

Martial law   The use of the military to impose control over a given area

Marxism   The thoughts of Karl Marx who was the founder of communism

Mechanisation   The use of machinery such as tractors to improve productivity

Menshevik   A member of one of the groups formed after the split in the Social Democratic Party in 1903. The Mensheviks (meaning 'minority') believed the Party should be a mass organisation, which all workers could join

Middle class   A social classification of people who are well educated, such as doctors, lawyers and teachers, who have good jobs and are neither very rich nor very poor

Military Revolutionary Committee (MRC)   A body originally set up by Social Revolutionaries and the Social Democrats to defend Russia against Germany and counter-revolution

Mutiny   Soldiers rebelling against their officers

National groups   A set of individuals whose identity is defined by a common country of nationality or national origin

Nepmen   Merchants/traders who became rich due to the New Economic Policy

New Economic Policy   Introduced in 1921 by Lenin to win back the support of the people. Allowed private businesses and farms and profit

NKVD   Name of secret police under Stalin

OGPU   The state security force which succeeded the *Cheka* (the Bolshevik secret police)

Old Bolsheviks   Original Bolshevik Party members under Lenin

Orthodox Church   Branch of Christianity, strong in Eastern Europe, established by a breakaway from the Catholic Church in the early Middle Ages

Party Congress   The meeting or gathering of members of the Communist Party

Party line   The views or ideas of a particular party

Permanent Revolution   In the eyes of Trotsky, this meant a world where somewhere a communist revolution was taking place and the old order was being overthrown, bringing in government by the people

Persecution   To mistreat an individual or group because of their race, class, political beliefs and/or religion

Politburo   The policy-making committee of the Communist Party in the Soviet Union

Pravda   The official Communist Party newspaper

Proletariat   The industrial working class

Proletkult   An organisation established after the October Revolution to provide the foundations for a truly proletarian art

Provisional Government   Temporary government set up after the abdication of Tsar Nicholas II

Purge   The systematic removal of enemies through terror

Red Army   The Soviet army

Red Guard   The Bolsheviks' own armed forces

Red International of the Trade Unions   An international organisation of revolutionary trade unions that existed between 1921 and 1937

Red (Great) Terror   A campaign of mass killings, torture and oppression by the *Cheka*

Republicanism   Supports the idea of a country being ruled by a republic with an elected president and parliament

Requisition brigades   Groups of the Red Army and the *Cheka* set up to seize food from the countryside

Revolution   A sudden and drastic change in a society's political, economic or cultural structures. Marx's view of a revolution was a violent overthrow of one system of production to the next, e.g. capitalism to socialism

Right wing   In this case, the less extreme communists who were prepared to accept some capitalist ideas

Romanov dynasty   Romanov was the family name of Tsar Nicholas. His family had ruled Russia since 1613

Russification   The policy of forcing non-Russians, such as Poles, to speak Russian and follow Russian customs

Sabotage   A deliberate act of destruction or obstruction

Saboteur   A person who deliberately destroys property

Separatist   A person who supports the separation of a particular group of people from a larger body on the basis of ethnicity, religion, or gender

Shock brigades   Groups of workers who were selected or volunteered for especially arduous tasks

Show trials   The trials of prominent politicians or opponents of the government, organised to demonstrate Stalin's power

Socialism   The belief that all means of production should be owned and run by the government for the benefit of everyone and that wealth should be divided equally

Socialist realism   The official art form under Stalin, which was supposed to show the real life of peasants and workers but was used to glorify Stalin and his achievements

Socialism in One Country   A policy put forward by Stalin which suggested that the Soviet Union should concentrate on securing communism at home before it supported revolution abroad

Socialist   Believer in the idea that there should be state ownership and control of the means of production, distribution and exchange

Socialist republics   Communist ruled areas which made up the Soviet Union

Soviet   An elected council of workers

Stakhanovites   Followers of Alexei Stakhanov (a miner, who, in the 1930s, had allegedly moved 102 tonnes of coal in one shift) who were dedicated to hard work

Subsistence farming   Producing just enough to live on with little or nothing left over to sell

Supreme Soviet   Soviets were local and regional workers' councils. Representatives from the regional soviets were sent to the Central or Supreme Soviet

Testament   Will

Tsarism   Refers to the system of government in Russia which was controlled by one man, the tsar

Universal education   Universal access to education is the ability of all people to have equal opportunity in education, regardless of their social class, gender, ethnicity background or physical and mental disabilities

Vesenkha   This was the Supreme Soviet of the National Economy, Superior Soviet of the People's Economy, set up after the October Revolution to manage the economy

War Communism   State control of industry and agriculture

Western Front   The main area of conflict in Western Europe during the First World War, with Britain, France and Belgium fighting against Germany

Whites   This was the name given to all those who opposed and fought against the Bolsheviks during the Civil War of 1918–21

Working class   Includes workers in industry, mainly in towns and cities

Zhenotdel   This was the department of the Russian Communist party devoted to women's affairs in the 1920s

Acknowledgements

The Publishers would like to thank the following for permission to reproduce copyright material:

Photo credits

p.4, **p.6**, **p.22**, **p.67**, **p.69** © Getty Images; **p.7**, **p.20**, **p.49**, **p.82**, **p.112**, **p.116**, **p.120** © Sovfoto/UIG/Getty Images; **p.8** *t*, **p.11** *b*, **p.25**, **p.34**, **p.73** *bl*, **p.89** © World History Archive/Alamy Stock Photo; **p.8** *b* © Imagno/Austrian Archives/TopFoto; **p.9**, **p.12** *tl*, **p.17**, **p.18**, **p.73** *ml*, *mr*, **p.97**, **p.107** © SPUTNIK/Alamy Stock Photo; **p.11** *t*, **p.30**, **p.76**, **p.78**, **p.79**, **p.88**, **p.100**, **p.106** © David King Collection, **p.12** *tr* © Gianni Dagli Orti/The Art Archive/Alamy Stock Photo; **p.12** *bl* © Tobie Mathew Collection/Bridgeman Images; **p.12** *br* © Topham Picturepoint; **p.15** © Getty/Hulton; **p.21**, **p.92**, **p.104**, **p.109** © ITAR-TASS Photo Agency/Alamy Stock Photo; **p.26** © Bulla/Slava Katamidze Collection/Getty Images; **p.27** © Ann Ronan Pictures/Print Collector/Getty Images; **p.29** © ITAR-TASS Photo Agency/TopFoto; **p.33** Keystone-France/Gamma-Rapho/Getty Images; **p.35**, **p.73** *tl* © Underwood Archives/Getty Images; **p.36** *r*, **p.39** © JT Vintage/Glasshouse Images/Alamy Stock Photo; **p.36** *l* © Granger, NYC/Alamy Stock Photo; **p.43** © Mary Evans Picture Library/Alamy Stock Photo; **p.44** © Hulton Archive/Getty Images; **p.52** © Pictorial Press Ltd/Alamy Stock Photo; **p.53** © DEA/G. DAGLI ORTI/Getty Images; **p.57**, **p.62** © Hoover Institute; **p.59** © ullstein bild/TopFoto; **p.60** © RIA Novosti/TopFoto; **p.64** © Fine Art Images/Superstock; **p.70** © SCRSS/TopFoto; **p.71**, **p.75** © James E. Abbe/ullstein bild/Getty Images; **p.73** *tr* © ullstein bild/Getty Images; **p.73** *br* © TopFoto; **p.81** © Bettmann/Getty Images; **p.84** © Berliner Verlag/DPA/PA Images; **p.79** © Everett Collection/Mary Evans; **p.89** © World History Archive/TopFoto; **p.90** Joeri De Rocker/Alamy Stock Photo; **p.91** © Memorial Art Gallery of the University of Rochester: Marion Stratton Gould; **p.93** © Fine Art Images/HIP/TopFoto; **p.101** © Photas/Tass/PA Images; **p.102** © Roger Perrin/The Bridgeman Art Library; **p.105** © Molly Riley/AFP/Getty Images; **p.111** *l* © Slava Katamidze Collection/Hulton Archive/Getty Images, *r* © Fine Art Images/Heritage Images/TopFoto; **p.114** © Universal History Archive/UIG/Getty Images; **p.115** © Danita Delimont/Getty Images; **p.117** *l* © DACS 2016/Sovfoto/UIG/Getty Images, *r* Internationaal Instituut voor Sociale Geschiedenis, Amsterdam; **p.118** © Heritage Image Partnership Ltd/Alamy Stock Photo.

Index